Early Praise for *More SQL Antipatterns*

Super relevant. Within a week of reading this book, I felt like a hero saving my team from the pagination antipattern. A Swiss army knife of database wisdom.

➤ **Marcus Adams**
Senior Software Developer

Having learned a lot of SQL tips from the first book of SQL antipatterns, I was very excited when Bill announced that he had just finished writing a new collection and wanted me to review it. The book is very well-written and easy to read. By reading this book, you will learn how to write better SQL queries, how to optimize them, and how to write your data access layer to get the best out of your relational database system. Therefore, if you are an application developer who uses an SQL database, you should definitely read both books of SQL antipatterns.

➤ **Vlad Mihalcea**
Java Champion and author of *High-Performance Java Persistence*

Bill is, in my experience, both incredibly knowledgeable about databases, and a very expert and wise software engineer. He passes along that expertise and wisdom in a very conversational way.

➤ **Steve Dinwiddie**
Vice President, Software Engineering

In this second volume, Bill continues to excel at identifying more SQL antipatterns found in present development practices. His clear explanations and the reasoning behind these corrections are an important skillset for anyone wanting to become an expert craftsperson in SQL.

➤ **Ronald Bradford**
Chief Technology Officer, ProxySQL

More SQL Antipatterns presents common challenges web developers face related to SQL and data access, helping them understand why a pattern is problematic and how to design a solution. The antipatterns are practical, showing how to build scalable pagination, restructure non-sargable queries, and when to denormalize, use semi-structured storage, or use caching. Even when working from an ORM, developers must understand efficient schema design, SQL query execution, and the effective use of indexes to build scalable and reliable systems. This book helps readers build those critical skills.

➤ **Andrew Atkinson**
author of *High Performance PostgreSQL for Rails*

One thing that sets experts apart is knowing antipatterns: what does not work, why, and what to do instead. You can take decades to learn SQL antipatterns, or you can read this book. I advise the latter.

➤ **Daniel Nichter**
DBA, author of *Efficient MySQL Performance*

This book is the perfect companion for any developer looking to step up their game when working with and designing for databases. The examples are fully applicable to any situation you might face in your day-to-day work—they'll have you nodding in recognition.

➤ **Laura Alcober Prieto**
Senior Software Engineer, Mercado Libre

Bill has a habit of seeing data sets in a way that most programmers don't. He shows examples of this change in viewpoint that look simple, but are, in fact, economical, elegant solutions that offer a world of benefit to both the developer and the code base.

➤ **Jan Dwyer**
Senior Programmer Analyst

More SQL Antipatterns

Avoid Common but Deadly Mistakes of Database Optimization

Bill Karwin

The Pragmatic Bookshelf

Dallas, Texas

See our complete catalog of hands-on, practical, and Pragmatic content for software developers:
https://pragprog.com

Sales, volume licensing, and support:
support@pragprog.com

Derivative works, AI training and testing, international translations, and other rights:
rights@pragprog.com

The team that produced this book includes:

Development Editor: Jacquelyn Carter
Copy Editor: Karen Galle

ISBN-13: 979-8-88865-206-0
Book version: P1.0—July, 2026

Contents

Part III — Application Design Antipatterns

Acknowledgments

I'd like to thank the thousands of software developers who asked their SQL questions on internet sites. It takes courage and humility to show your mistakes in public. I'm indebted to them for doing so because it gave me the opportunity to hone my knowledge of SQL and practice my ability to write clearly. Education and practice are both necessary to build skills, but the very best way to learn a subject is to teach it to someone else.

I'm honored that the following technical reviewers offered their time and comments on the book's draft: Marcus Adams, Laura Alcober Prieto, Ronald Bradford, Steve Dinwiddie, Vlad Mihalcea, Daniel Nichter, and Markus Winand. All their feedback made the book better. Thank you!

Thank you to my publisher Dave Thomas and my editor Jacquelyn Carter, who believed in this book enough to give me the opportunity to write it.

My deepest thanks to my wife Jan Dwyer, who is an accomplished writer and a database developer in her own right. She was the first reviewer of every chapter of this book. Her perspective has been invaluable, but her consistent support, encouragement, and inspiration were what made me able to finish this project.

Preface

I couldn't have predicted how writing my first book on SQL antipatterns in 2010 would launch me into an adventure as an SQL performance consultant, trainer, and database developer and administrator.

I visited dozens of companies, small and large, where I saw similar struggles to optimize their MySQL-based web projects. I developed and presented training for hundreds of top developers, helping them rise to the next level of creating world-class applications. I administered databases for the notification service used by the majority of schools in the United States and Canada, and at a trendy digital financial services company. I optimized SQL code and operations that processed millions of transactions per hour.

During this time, I stayed engaged with the software developer community by volunteering to answer over 8,500 questions about SQL on Stack Overflow. My contributions were viewed 56 million times.[1]

Those years of work gave me a lot of insight into the types of problems SQL developers face all over the world. Now, I want to share what I've learned in my career, going deeper into SQL in this new volume.

Who This Book Is For

More SQL Antipatterns is for any software developer who needs to use SQL—which is virtually all software developers. It doesn't matter whether you're a beginner or a seasoned professional. People at all levels of experience will benefit from the subjects in this book.

You may have read a reference on SQL syntax. Now you know all the clauses of a SELECT statement, and you can get some work done. Gradually, you increase your SQL skills by reading code, books, and blogs. In spite of this, it's hard to tell if you're learning best practices or another way to paint yourself into a corner.

1. https://stackoverflow.com/users/20860/bill-karwin

You may find some topics in *More SQL Antipatterns* are well-known to you. You'll see new ways of looking at the problems, even if you're already aware of the solutions. It's good to reinforce your good practices by reviewing widespread programmer misconceptions and the reasons we avoid them.

If you're a DBA, this book can help you explain good practices to the software developers you work with and the consequences of straying from that path. It's not uncommon for the relationship between developers and database administrators to be contentious, and hopefully, you'll gain some material that can be used for a common understanding with your colleagues.

What's in This Book

Each chapter focuses on one antipattern. You can more or less read the chapters in any order.

In addition, you'll find *mini-antipatterns* throughout the book, following each chapter. These cover other mistakes commonly made by developers using SQL. Mini-antipatterns are covered more briefly than the main antipatterns.

Many of the antipattern chapters have humorous or evocative titles. It's traditional to give both positive design patterns and antipatterns names that serve as a metaphor or mnemonic.

The appendixes provide practical descriptions of some relational database theory.

Do You Need to Read Volume 1 First?

I re-released my earlier book in 2022 with updates and additional topics, as *SQL Antipatterns Volume 1: Avoiding the Pitfalls of Database Programming.* [Kar22]

The book you're holding contains all new topics. Rather than repeat any of the content of that book, I'll make references to topics in *SQL Antipatterns, Volume 1*, with the assumption that you have access to the prior book.

I hope this gives both books distinct value, and both stand on their own. You can get what you need out of either one without needing to own the other, but if you have both books on your shelf, they both deserve their place.

What's Not in This Book

There are plenty of books and internet resources for the basics of the SQL language, so this book assumes the reader has learned enough SQL syntax already to use the language and get some work done. Recommended books for learning basic SQL include:

- *Learning SQL: Generate, Manipulate, and Retrieve Data, 3rd Edition [Bea20]*
- *SQL in a Nutshell: A Desktop Quick Reference, 4th Edition [KOH22]*
- *SQL Queries for Mere Mortals: A Hands-On Guide to Data Manipulation in SQL, 4th Edition [Vie18]*

Performance, scalability, and optimization are important topics for database-driven applications, especially on the web, but it's not the main focus of this book. Recommended books specifically about performance and scalability include:

- *High Performance PostgreSQL for Rails [Atk24]*
- *Effective MySQL Optimizing SQL Statements [Bra11]*
- *High-Performance Java Persistence [Mih16]*
- *Efficient MySQL Performance [Nic21]*
- *SQL Performance Explained [Win12]*

Every brand of SQL database product has its own tools and commands, but this book is not a command reference or a collection of recipes.

Database administration and operation tasks such as server sizing, capacity planning, installation and configuration, monitoring, backups, log analysis, and security are important and deserve a book of their own.

Conventions in This Book

The following sections describe some conventions in this book.

Typography

SQL keywords are formatted in all capitals and in a monospaced font to make them stand out from the text, as in `SELECT`. SQL tables, also in a monospaced font, are spelled with a capital for the initial letter of each word in the table name, as in `Accounts` or `BugsProducts`. SQL columns, also in a monospaced font, are spelled in lowercase, and words are separated by underscores, as in `account_name`.

Literal strings are formatted in italics, as in *bill@example.com*.

Terminology

SQL is pronounced "ess-cue-ell," not "see-quell." Both usages are common enough that everyone will know what you mean. In this book, the former is used. You will read phrases like "*an* SQL query," not "*a* SQL query."

In this book, the plural of *index* is *indexes*. In other contexts, it may be pluralized as *indices*. Both are correct according to most dictionaries.

In SQL, the terms *query* and *statement* are somewhat interchangeable, being any complete SQL command that you can execute. In this book, for the sake of clarity, *query* refers to SELECT statements and *statement* refers to all others.

Online Resources

The examples and source code shown in this book are under the source code link on the Pragmatic Bookshelf website.[2] You can also report any errors or suggestions using the errata link on the same site.

If you like this book and it serves you well, I hope that you will let others know about it—your reviews really do help.

Let's get into it!

2. https://pragprog.com/book/bksap2

You must learn from the mistakes of others—you will never live long enough to make them all yourself.

Anonymous

CHAPTER 1

Why SQL?

Why are we still developing software with SQL?

Recently, SQL turned 50. It was first developed at IBM in the early 1970s, and it quickly became a popular solution for structured data programming. Many software companies developed their own implementations of SQL. An ANSI standard was published in 1986 and adopted by ISO in 1987. Since then, it has been revised many times, most recently in 2023.

Software application needs are very different from those in the 1970s or 1980s. Is a technology so old even relevant anymore? Aren't more recent languages more suited to modern software development?

Let's take a look.

SQL Is Ubiquitous

SQL is based on an innovative computer science theory published in the 1970 paper *A Relational Model of Data for Large Shared Data Banks [Cod70]* by E. F. Codd. This method has allowed software developers to store and retrieve data with a powerful declarative language while maintaining the integrity of a custom data model. Every attempt to replace SQL has sacrificed either the versatility of the query language or the stability of the data model, or both. Calling relational theory outdated would be like saying Boolean algebra is outdated.

SQL has been a resilient part of the software developer's toolset for decades. The annual Stack Overflow surveys from 2017–2025[1] report that SQL is used more than almost any other programming language (JavaScript and sometimes

1. https://survey.stackoverflow.co

Python are ahead of SQL). The TIOBE Programming Community Index[2] measures popularity differently, but still ranks SQL in the top 10 languages.

SQL works with every popular programming language, from older compiled languages like C, C++, Java, and C#, to dynamic languages such as PHP, Ruby, Python, and JavaScript, to newer languages such as Go and Rust. SQL is complementary to all languages, rather than being a competitor.

An abundance of supporting technologies are designed to work with SQL, including editors, debuggers, code generators, and object mapping libraries. Naturally, none of these technologies work with any alternative, and it wouldn't be good business for the makers of these products to try to add support for the alternatives when SQL is so popular.

SQL isn't always the best solution for a specific case, but it's the best at satisfying a broad variety of cases. You could invent a bespoke data management solution tailored to a specific application, and that solution might be better for that application than SQL. But if you're the only one who knows your homegrown solution, it'll be hard for your business to hire new programmers who can understand it quickly and use it to work efficiently. Reinventing a wheel that is already very well made and well known usually hinders your success rather than helps it.

One reason we use SQL is that it is standard, and that itself has value.

Does AI Make Learning SQL Obsolete?

Virtually all software developers are now using LLM tools to assist writing code. When used properly, this has become a game changer for the productivity of programmers.

If this tool is available to us today, does anyone need to learn to program in SQL again? SQL, in particular, being so mature and well-known, seems like a perfect candidate for automating with an LLM.

NVIDIA CEO Jensen Huang said at the World Government Summit in February 2024:[3]

> It is our job to create technology such that nobody has to program. And that the programming language is human. Everybody in the world is now a programmer. This is the miracle of artificial intelligence.

---

2. https://www.tiobe.com/tiobe-index/
3. https://www.youtube.com/watch?v=8Pm2xEViNIo

That is at least the promise of LLM tools, but it's still quite far from being a reality. The experiences of software developers who have tried using LLMs to write code for significantly complex projects have discovered two things about these tools.

First, LLM's are impressive for some tasks, but the nature of these tools is that they only *mimic* content based on statistical similarity. They don't understand how code works, or even what your request means. The current developer experience with LLM's is that, unless the request is very simple, an LLM may respond with nonworking code or an inaccurate or inefficient implementation of the desired application. In some cases, the LLM generates code including invalid syntax, resembling the programming language but not, in fact, working or matching legal syntax. These nonsensical results from LLMs have been called "hallucinations." Google CEO Sundar Pichai said in a May 2024 interview about LLM's:[4]

> Hallucination is still an unsolved problem. In some ways, it's an inherent feature.

It's great to use an LLM, but its output must be reviewed by a trained software developer to make sure it does what is intended, and to understand it well enough to discard failures and try again. Research by Uplevel in 2023–2024 concluded that code generated using the LLM tool Copilot had 41 percent more bugs than code written by human software developers and did not change productivity metrics significantly.[5] Perhaps LLM code generation will improve in the future, but it clearly has a long way to go.

A technical writer colleague of mine described her principle for getting engineers to talk about their software: "you can't get the right answers until you ask the right questions." The same is true of LLM's. We call this *prompt engineering*, or describing the request with enough unambiguous detail and specificity that the LLM is constrained to produce a working solution. Eventually, people who practice prompt engineering must decompose problems in exactly the same way that programmers do when they write code, and the language they use to express prompts for the LLM must become as precise and meticulous as traditional coding languages. The dream of describing software in a layperson's language will never come true, except for very simple programs.

Second, LLM's aren't able to create novel solutions. They only synthesize from what they've been trained on, and they're limited by the quality and variety

---

4. https://www.theverge.com/24158374/google-ceo-sundar-pichai-ai-search-gemini-future-of-the-internet-web-openai-decoder-interview
5. https://resources.uplevelteam.com/gen-ai-for-coding

of their training data. This means there is a constant demand for new, high-quality examples, written by human experts, to use to train the LLM. There are even people employed to write code, not for software projects, but for feeding directly to an LLM.

LLM tools make programmers more productive for some tasks, but they don't replace human programmers or make their knowledge obsolete.

SQL remains one of the most widely used technologies.

If you develop software—with LLM assistance or with traditional methods—you need to understand how to use SQL effectively.

What Is an Antipattern?

Everyone makes mistakes, but experts try to learn from their mistakes, turning them into opportunities to improve their skills. You can become a better software developer by studying the most common errors made by other developers and learning how to fix them.

An *antipattern* is a technique that is intended to solve a problem, but that often leads to other problems. An antipattern is practiced widely in different ways, but with a thread of commonality. People may independently come up with an idea that fits an antipattern or do so with help from a colleague, a book, or an article. Many antipatterns of object-oriented software design and project management are documented at the Portland Pattern Repository,[6] as well as in the 1998 book *AntiPatterns [BMMM98]*.

Antipatterns are the opposite of *patterns*, the term we use for recurring solutions that can be applied in many software projects. Each situation is unique, but the solutions are similar. The same is true for antipatterns—these are mistakes that are used in different projects, due to common misconceptions, and with the same undesirable results.

More SQL Antipatterns describes the most frequent missteps software developers naively make while using SQL. I have talked to them in technical support and training sessions, worked alongside them developing software, and answered their questions on internet forums. Many of these blunders I've made myself; there's no better teacher than spending many hours late at night making up for one's own errors.

6. https://wiki.c2.com/?AntiPattern

Types of Antipatterns

The chapters are organized into three parts for the following categories of antipatterns:

SQL Language Antipatterns
: Some problems are due to misunderstanding the usage of the SQL language, or trying to do uncommon tasks. This section includes several types of SQL queries that developers struggle with.

SQL Optimization Antipatterns
: As the saying goes, "make it work, make it right, then make it fast." An SQL query may work, but it doesn't necessarily come with optimal performance. It's important to be mindful of methods to optimize queries.

Application Design Antipatterns
: SQL is supposed to be used in the context of applications written in another language, such as C++, Java, PHP, Python, or Ruby. There are right ways and wrong ways to employ SQL in an application, and this part of the book describes some common blunders.

Anatomy of an Antipattern

Each antipattern chapter contains the following subheadings:

Objective
: This is the task that you may be trying to solve. Antipatterns are used with the intention to provide that solution, but they end up causing more problems than they solve.

The Antipattern
: This section describes the nature of the common solution and illustrates the unforeseen consequences that make it an antipattern.

How to Recognize the Antipattern
: There may be certain clues that help you identify when an antipattern is being used in your project. Certain types of barriers you encounter, or quotes you may hear yourself or others saying, can tip you off to the presence of an antipattern.

Legitimate Uses of the Antipattern
: Rules usually have exceptions. There may be circumstances in which an approach normally considered an antipattern is nevertheless appropriate, or at least the lesser of all evils.

Solution

This section describes the preferred solutions, which solve the original objective without running into the problems caused by the antipattern.

Example Database

Most examples in this book are based on the database-access code in a hypothetical social media web application called Visage.

Visage uses PostgreSQL 18.1 for its database. The application code is written in Python 3.14, except in Chapter 8, NoSQL: The Grass Is Always Greener, on page 87 because the connector for Cassandra requires Python 3.11. Visage code uses Flask 3.1.2, psycopg2 2.9.11, and SQLAlchemy 2.0.44.

The following data definition language shows the tables defined in SQL. In some cases, choices are made for the sake of examples later in the book, so they might not always be the choices one would make in a real-world application. Examples use only standard SQL, so they are applicable to any brand of database, but some PostgreSQL data types also appear, such as SERIAL.

The naming convention in the Visage project is:

- Identifiers are lowercase.
- Words in identifiers are separated with underscores (_).
- Identifier delimiters are not used unless needed. For example, a table name that matches an SQL reserved keyword, like "user", is delimited in double-quotes.
- Table names are singular nouns.

Introduction/visage.sql

```
CREATE TABLE user_type (
  user_type_id SMALLSERIAL PRIMARY KEY,
  user_type VARCHAR(16) NOT NULL
);

CREATE TABLE "user" (
  user_id BIGSERIAL PRIMARY KEY,
  user_type_id SMALLINT NOT NULL REFERENCES user_type,
  display_name VARCHAR(64) NOT NULL,
  real_name VARCHAR(64) NOT NULL,
  thumbnail BYTEA,
  contact_email VARCHAR(64) NOT NULL,
  contact_phone VARCHAR(64) NOT NULL,
  birth_date DATE
);
```

```
CREATE TABLE tag (
  tag_id SERIAL PRIMARY KEY,
  tag TEXT NOT NULL
);

CREATE TABLE post (
  post_id BIGSERIAL PRIMARY KEY,
  post_title TEXT NOT NULL,
  post_text TEXT NOT NULL,
  user_id BIGINT NOT NULL REFERENCES "user",
  view_count BIGINT NOT NULL DEFAULT 0,
  created_at TIMESTAMP NOT NULL DEFAULT CURRENT_TIMESTAMP,
  updated_at TIMESTAMP NOT NULL DEFAULT CURRENT_TIMESTAMP,
  notified_at TIMESTAMP NULL
);

CREATE TABLE post_tag (
  post_id BIGINT REFERENCES post,
  tag_id INT REFERENCES TAG,
  PRIMARY KEY (post_id, tag_id)
);

CREATE TABLE comment (
  comment_id BIGSERIAL PRIMARY KEY,
  post_id BIGINT NOT NULL REFERENCES post,
  comment_text TEXT NOT NULL,
  in_reply_to BIGINT REFERENCES comment,
  user_id BIGINT NOT NULL REFERENCES "user",
  created_at TIMESTAMP NOT NULL DEFAULT CURRENT_TIMESTAMP,
  notified_at TIMESTAMP NULL
);

CREATE TABLE rating (
  post_id BIGINT REFERENCES post,
  user_id BIGINT REFERENCES "user",
  rating NUMERIC NOT NULL CHECK (rating BETWEEN 0 AND 5),
  PRIMARY KEY (post_id, user_id)
);
```

Indexes are recommended to optimize queries in a real application, but to keep examples simpler in this book, indexes are not shown.

The Visage database can also be shown as the entity-relationship diagram on the following page.

This diagram was designed using DBeaver 25.1.0, an open source database developer's tool.[7]

In some chapters, different database definitions appear, either to exhibit an antipattern or to show an alternative solution that avoids the antipattern.

7. https://dbeaver.io/

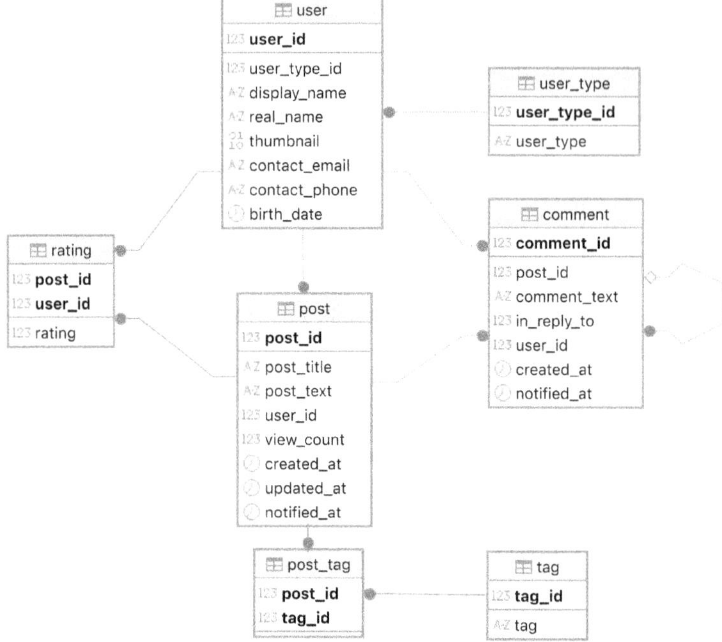

What's Next

Now that you've seen the case for SQL as a fundamental skill for all software developers, you're prepared to read the rest of this book. You'll see many common mistakes made with SQL—antipatterns we should look out for.

Next, we'll dive into each antipattern, discover the trouble they cause for our example application, and find out how to get ourselves out of that trouble.

Part I

SQL Language Antipatterns

Some problems are due to misunderstanding usage of the SQL language, or trying to do uncommon tasks. This section includes several types of SQL queries that developers struggle with.

Indeed it has been said that democracy is the worst form of government except for all those other forms that have been tried from time to time.

Winston Churchill

CHAPTER 2

Fear of JOINs

Oliver, a senior Java programmer, was struggling to get some code written. He was behind on his deadline. I asked him what he was trying to do and if I could help.

He said he needed data from two tables. He needed all data from the first table and only the matching data from the second table. Where there was no matching data, he still wanted the data from the first table, but with nulls for the objects where there was no match in the second table.

"What's the problem? That's an outer join in SQL," I replied.

Oliver said he didn't know how to use an outer join, so he had spent many hours trying to code the task from scratch using Java. He was fetching all the data from both tables, matching it up, and discarding data from the second dataset that didn't match. He was trying to make the matching more efficient by implementing Java classes to collect the results into a B-tree data structure.

"No, really, the database can do that easily," I offered. "It'll run faster, require less code, and you'll only fetch the results of the match. I'll show you how."

Oliver's face grew dark, and he said to me, "I *forbid* you from showing me an outer join!"

He had invested so much in implementing his data structure that he couldn't bear to admit he had wasted his time. He finished his pages of Java code, and never learned how to do the same task in one line of SQL.

Objective: Combining Matching Data in Two Tables

Every software developer wants to write code that is simple, efficient, and free of bugs.

Typically, you design a database properly using the *rules of normalization*. This method of relational data organization helps to prevent data anomalies by storing each fact as a row in one place. This means that sets of facts are frequently stored as multiple rows in multiple tables, and some types of queries must cross-reference sets of rows from the multiple tables to ensure they match. This is a *join*.

A join is a different kind of operation than software developers usually work with. It isn't a loop. It isn't a function call. It isn't an object-oriented operation or a recursion. A join is an operation to match elements of two sets that relate to one another. This is powerful, but it can be confusing because it's unfamiliar. It also needs to be done with care, making sure it can be run efficiently on large sets.

What's the best way to gain the advantage of normalized data organization, and also write optimized queries?

Antipattern: Fearing JOINs

Software developers may have had bad experiences with queries that aren't optimized well. These developers conclude that any join operation is inefficient, and they should avoid using joins at all.

Developers who decide that they must avoid joins force themselves to write code using alternative methods, even if these duplicate the work of a join in a less efficient way. The following sections describe some common choices for these alternatives.

Suppose you have a feature to implement in the Visage application to show a thread of a user's comments. For each comment, you must also show details of the user who posted that comment, such as their name, a thumbnail image, and the type of user.

Let's look at a few ways developers try to code this type of query, if they assume they must avoid using JOIN.

Subqueries in the WHERE Clause

One popular alternative to a join is to compare rows to a subquery in a WHERE clause. Some developers have a more intuitive feel for subqueries than they do for joins because subqueries resemble nested loops.

Here are two examples that use subqueries to give similar results:

JOIN/anti/subquery-in.sql
```
SELECT * FROM comment
WHERE user_id IN (SELECT user_id FROM "user");
```

JOIN/anti/subquery-exists.sql

```
SELECT * FROM comment
WHERE EXISTS (
  SELECT * FROM "user"
  WHERE "user".user_id = comment.user_id
);
```

The latter example is called a *correlated subquery* because the subquery has a condition in its WHERE clause that restricts the row it returns to those that match the row of the outer query when the subquery is called. The SQL engine may execute the subquery many times, once for each row of the outer query. This will degrade performance.

Besides performance, these solutions have the limitation that columns from the subquery can't be included in the result of the outer query. Only columns of tables referenced in the outer query can be included in the *select-list* (the list of columns or expressions following the SELECT keyword in a query).

This solution is useful if the goal was only to restrict the rows returned by the first table, but it is not useful if the result must include columns from both tables.

Correlated Subqueries in the Select-List

If the columns of the joined table are needed in the query result, another work-around is to use subquery expressions in the select-list. This must be done one column at a time, so it requires you to do a lot of repetitive typing, and it makes the whole SQL query appear lengthy.

JOIN/anti/subquery-select-list.sql

```
SELECT comment.*,
  (SELECT display_name FROM "user"
    WHERE "user".user_id = comment.user_id) AS user_name,
  (SELECT thumbnail FROM "user"
    WHERE "user".user_id = comment.user_id) AS thumbnail,
  (SELECT user_type_id FROM "user"
    WHERE "user".user_id = comment.user_id) AS user_type_id
FROM comment;
```

The select-list can only include scalar expressions, that is, expressions that consist of a single value. The subquery returns one column, so you have to repeat the whole subquery expression for each column you need. You're not allowed to query multiple columns or to use SELECT * in a scalar subquery.

JOIN/anti/subquery-select-list-multi-column.sql

```
SELECT comment.*,       -- INVALID because the subquery returns multiple columns
  (SELECT display_name, thumbnail, user_type_id FROM "user"
    WHERE "user".user_id = comment.user_id) AS user_columns
FROM comment;
```

This returns the following error:

```
ERROR:  subquery must return only one column
```

A scalar subquery must return a single value, not values from multiple rows. This means it can work if the table in the outer query has a many-to-one relationship with the table in the subquery, but not if it's a one-to-many relationship. Suppose in this example, the user table is queried by the outer table, and the subqueries fetch columns from the comment table. Each user may have made many comments, in which case the subquery returns multiple rows. This is not valid as a scalar subquery.

JOIN/anti/subquery-select-list-multi-row.sql

```
-- INVALID because the subquery may return multiple rows
SELECT "user".*,
  (SELECT comment_text FROM comment
    WHERE comment.user_id = "user".user_id) AS comment_text,
  (SELECT created_at FROM comment
    WHERE comment.user_id = "user".user_id) AS created_at,
  (SELECT in_reply_to FROM comment
    WHERE comment.user_id = "user".user_id) AS in_reply_to
FROM "user";
```

This returns the following error:

```
ERROR:  more than one row returned by a subquery used as an expression
```

Client-Side Join

In the story at the start of this chapter, a developer had a task that should have been solved by a type of join, but he assumed that doing separate queries against his two tables would be simpler or more efficient.

His application had to run two queries to fetch all the rows from both tables, so he could compare the rows one by one in the application. Reading all the rows of a table instead of only the subset of rows your query needs is called a *full table-scan.* As you add rows, the performance gets slower and slower, in direct proportion to the table size. Every row read from the table takes a little bit of work, and if the table has thousands or millions of rows, this adds up.

The following Python script shows an implementation of a client-side join. It runs two separate queries, each against a single table, which return the full set of rows from each table. Then it loops over these sets, merging the matching user rows into the comment rows.

JOIN/anti/client-side-join.py

```
import psycopg2
import psycopg2.extras

conn = psycopg2.connect("dbname='visage' host='localhost'")

with conn.cursor(cursor_factory=psycopg2.extras.RealDictCursor) as cur:

    users = dict()
    cur.execute("""
        SELECT user_id, display_name
        FROM "user"
        """)

    # Transform result into dict, keyed by user_id.
    # The Java developer in the story implemented this
    # by coding a B-tree from scratch.
    for row in cur:
        user_id = row['user_id']
        users[user_id] = row

    cur.execute("""
        SELECT comment_id, comment_text, in_reply_to,
            user_id, created_at
        FROM comment
        """)
    comments = cur.fetchall()

# Match rows from each set together, and make combined rows.
for comment in comments:
    if comment['user_id'] in users:
        user = users[comment['user_id']]
        comment.update(user)

print(comments)
```

The client-side join is bad for performance and efficiency for at least two reasons.

First, the entire dataset needs to be held in Python's memory. The risk is that even if it works today while you develop and test your application, as the data grows in the database, eventually it'll be more than the client can hold.

Second, data needs to be held by the client even if it's not referenced. For example, if there are a thousand users in the database, but only fifty who have written comments, then 95 percent of the rows fetched by the user's query are not needed. All the rows need to be fetched because you don't know which ones are referenced by comments until after the client-side join is done.

N+1 Queries

Some developers execute one query against a single table, then for each row returned by the first query, execute an additional query to fetch related rows from a second table. This avoids using JOIN, but it results in a great increase in the number of SQL queries to run. Since there is always at least one query that returns N rows of results, and therefore N queries follow, this practice is called an "N+1 query." See Mini-Antipattern: N+1 Queries, on page 98 for an example.

Network Bandwidth Cost

This is an additional problem that applies to the previous two practices, client-side joins and N+1 queries.

When a query fetches its results, those rows are transmitted over the network from the database to the application. Modern networks are quite fast, but their speed is not limitless. If you try to move a large enough result set over a network, the transfer time may be more than you want.

For example, if a row is 200 bytes and your network has a bandwidth of 1 gigabit per second, then transferring 1 million rows takes 1 million * 200 * 8 bits/byte divided by 1 billion bits per second, which works out to at least 1.6 seconds. That time alone could be more than your application's required response time, and it's only the network transfer time for one query. Some applications need to run several queries to make a full response, and there may be many such requests at the same time, putting further pressure on the bandwidth.

It's wasteful and inefficient to consume so much network bandwidth unnecessarily. This increases the performance cost of your queries, and ultimately, your application.

Organizing Data Differently

Some developers store data in alternative ways that don't require using JOIN. For example, data that would be stored in two tables in a normalized database design could be combined into one table, as if they were already joined. These are covered in more detail later in this book, in Chapter 7, Premature Denormalization, on page 67, Chapter 8, NoSQL: The Grass Is Always Greener, on page 87, and Chapter 9, JSON: Matryoshka Dolls, on page 101.

How to Recognize the Antipattern

- "We don't use joins because we heard they are slow."

Certainly, unoptimized queries can have poor performance, whether they involve joins or not. But once the right indexes are built to support the join, a query can run them with good performance.

- "How can I find a value in a table depending on a value in a different table?"

  Developers who are new to SQL may describe in their own terms the result of a join, without realizing that's what it's called or how to run one.

- "I need to find rows in table1 that have no match in table2."

  Join is flexible and powerful. Thinking of joined tables in terms of sets of rows, you can write queries that do more than simply match rows.

Legitimate Uses of the Antipattern

The subquery solution with EXISTS that you saw in the antipattern section has a legitimate use. It can be used to implement a *semi-join*, which is a query that returns the rows from one table only once, even if there are multiple matches in the second table. The result is not multiplied by the number of matches in the joined table.

Likewise, using separate queries is necessary when the tables to be joined reside on different database instances. Typically, one database instance can only see data stored in that instance, and that's where the SQL query is executed. You can run the query in either instance, but neither can join with data from the other instance. It may be that the only way to combine data from two instances is to run a query against each, fetch the results, and combine them in your application. A good tip in this case is to run both queries to sort the results by the columns you wish to join on, then fetch rows from a cursor one at a time, skipping past nonmatching rows. You still have to examine rows of each table that won't be included in the result, but you don't have to store the full result set in the client.

There's an example on the next page.

JOIN/soln/client-side-join-collated.py

```
import psycopg2
import psycopg2.extras

# Pretend these are two different database servers.
conn1 = psycopg2.connect("dbname='visage' host='localhost'")
conn2 = psycopg2.connect("dbname='visage' host='localhost'")

cur1 = conn1.cursor(cursor_factory=psycopg2.extras.RealDictCursor)
cur2 = conn2.cursor(cursor_factory=psycopg2.extras.RealDictCursor)

cur1.execute("""
    SELECT user_id, display_name
    FROM "user"
    ORDER BY user_id
    """)

cur2.execute("""
    SELECT comment_id, comment_text, in_reply_to,
        user_id, created_at
    FROM comment
    ORDER BY user_id
    """)

# Initial user dict has a user_id 0, which is a number
# but does not match any user_id referenced by any comment.
user = {"user_id": 0}

for comment in cur2:
    # Skip over users until the cursor reaches a user that matches
    # the current comment.
    while (user["user_id"] < comment["user_id"]):
        user = cur1.fetchone()
    comment.update(user)
    print(comment)
```

It's okay to run separate queries if the respective sets of matching rows have no logical relationship to each other. It's not necessary to do all your database work in a single query, and keeping unrelated queries separate is better for efficiency and code design.

Solution: Preferring JOINs

The best way to employ the power and efficiency of SQL is to use operations like join to give you an advantage. The following section describes the basic concepts of joins and explains how it solves the problems described earlier in this chapter.

Thinking in Sets

The task for the Visage application earlier in this chapter was to join comments to the respective details of the user who posted the comment. This is how you write that as a join in SQL:

JOIN/soln/simple-join.sql
```
SELECT *
FROM comment
JOIN "user" ON comment.user_id = "user".user_id;
```

SQL is a declarative language. You don't have to write code to loop over rows or look up matching rows. You should think of a table as a set of rows, and each row may match a set of rows from the other joined table.

You write a simple join as references to two tables, with a conditional expression. Rows from each table are compared, and if the condition is true for a given pairing of rows, then these rows are joined and become included in the query result. Let's look at an example.

The figure on the next page shows a join in action.

At the top are two tables, comment and user. The table at the bottom is the result of joining the two tables. The result table contains data from both of the original tables: data from the users table is selected based on the user_id column in the comment table.

The following example shows how you can write further filtering conditions in the WHERE clause, or expressions in the select-list, that reference columns that originated in both tables.

JOIN/soln/simple-join-where.sql
```
SELECT comment.comment_id, comment.comment_text,
  CURRENT_TIMESTAMP - comment.created_at AS age,
  "user".user_id, "user".display_name
FROM comment
JOIN "user" ON comment.user_id = "user".user_id
WHERE comment.created_at > CURRENT_TIMESTAMP - INTERVAL '7' DAY
  AND "user".user_type_id = 2;
```

A given row from one table might have many matches in the joined table. Each of these pairings is included in the set of results. At first, it might seem funny or repetitive that the row from one table appears multiple times in the join result when it has multiple matches in the joined table, but the rows of the result are actually still unique, if you look at the combined set of columns.

"comment"

comment_id	comment_text	in_reply_to	user_id
1	Well, let's see, we have on the St Louis team, Who's on first, What's on second, I Don't Know is on third...	NULL	1
2	That's what I want to find out.	1	2
3	I say Who's on first, What's on second, I Don't Know's on third.	2	1
4	Are you the manager?	3	2
5	Yes.	4	1
6	You gonna be the coach too?	5	2
7	Yes.	6	1
8	And you don't know the fellows' names?	7	2
9	Well I should.	8	1
10	Well then who's on first?	9	2
11	Yes.	10	1

"user"

user_id	real_name	contact_email
1	Bud	bud@visage.example
2	Lou	lou@visage.example
3	Groucho	groucho@visage.example
4	Chico	chico@visage.example
5	Harpo	harpo@visage.example

"comment" JOIN "user"

comment_id	comment_text	in_reply_to	user_id	real_name	contact_email
1	Well, let's see, we have on the St Louis team, Who's on first, What's on second, I Don't Know is on third...	NULL	1	Bud	bud@visage.example
2	That's what I want to find out.	1	2	Lou	lou@visage.example
3	I say Who's on first, What's on second, I Don't Know's on third.	2	1	Bud	bud@visage.example
4	Are you the manager?	3	2	Lou	lou@visage.example
5	Yes.	4	1	Bud	bud@visage.example
6	You gonna be the coach too?	5	2	Lou	lou@visage.example
7	Yes.	6	1	Bud	bud@visage.example
8	And you don't know the fellows' names?	7	2	Lou	lou@visage.example
9	Well I should.	8	1	Bud	bud@visage.example
10	Well then who's on first?	9	2	Lou	lou@visage.example
11	Yes.	10	1	Bud	bud@visage.example

In a relational database, each table is a *relation*—a set of rows where every row has the same columns. The result of joining two relations is itself also a relation. That allows the result of any join to be used in further relational operations.

JOIN Fixes All the Problems

Once you use a join, the problems shown earlier in the chapter are solved.

Subqueries in the WHERE clause:

- There are no subqueries, so it avoids the problem of correlated subqueries.
- You can include columns from both tables in the query result.

Subqueries in the select-list:

- There are no subqueries, so you can write your query more clearly and concisely.

Client-side join:

- You can get the result with just one query, instead of a query per table.
- You don't have to write custom code to sort and merge the results. The SQL engine takes care of that and returns the result of the join.
- It avoids holding the entire contents of both tables in memory on the client.

N+1 queries:

- You can get the result with just one query, instead of a query per row.

Network bandwidth cost:

- The join happens in the SQL engine, so only the result is transferred over the network.
- The network usage is typically reduced, at least if the matching rows are a subset of each table.

How Do You Join More Tables?

A join combines two relations, and the result is a new relation, which you can use in another join or other relational operations.

Compare this to arithmetic. A binary operation like addition combines two numbers, for instance $x + y$. The result is another number, which you can use in further operations: $(x + y) + z$. You can compose long and complex arithmetic expressions if you do it one operation at a time.

The same is true of joins. You can build complex queries that join many tables by adding one table at a time and trying the query at each stage to make sure it's producing the result you want. Then treat the result as a new relation, which you join to one more table.

Optimizing Joins

You do need to take care to optimize queries with joins, just as you would optimize any other query. Indexes are the most common way to do this. See the chapter "Index Shotgun" in *SQL Antipatterns Volume 1 [Kar22]*.

Most SQL engines implement *nested-loop joins* because it's a versatile way of evaluating a wide variety of types of joins. You can think of these just like a nested loop in your favorite programming language. In pseudocode, you can visualize this:

```
for each row in first joined table:
  for each matching row in the second joined table:
    yield joined row
```

The lookup in the nested part works just like a lookup in a simple, non-join query; the lookup uses an index if it can. If it cannot use an index to make that lookup efficient, it may have to scan the entire joined table for each row of the first table.

Make sure that joins are supported by an appropriate index—the same index you would use for a lookup. In the simple join example you saw in Thinking in Sets, on page 19, the index should begin with the `user.user_id` column because that's how the rows are looked up for each respective row of the `comment` table. In this case, that column is the primary key of the `user` table, so it's bound to be indexed already.

Many SQL products also implement a *hash join*, which works differently than nested-loop joins. This builds a temporary hash table of rows from one side of the join, after filtering the rows using other conditions of the `WHERE` clause. This avoids repeated lookups into the table, as the nested-loop join does. A hash join is a good optimization, but it only works for equality join conditions. The SQL engine should employ a hash join automatically when it's advantageous.

When supported by an appropriate index, a join isn't as costly for performance as some people fear.

Avoiding joins is like avoiding loops in your application code.

Mini-Antipattern: Comma-Style Join Syntax

You might see examples of SQL queries that use a different syntax for joins. The following two queries do the same thing:

```
SELECT * FROM comment, "user"
WHERE comment.user_id = "user".user_id;

SELECT * FROM comment
JOIN "user" ON comment.user_id = "user".user_id;
```

The former syntax was in the SQL-89 standard, and the latter was in the SQL-92 standard. The old style has been obsolete for many years, but it's still preserved for backward compatibility in most SQL implementations (Snowflake is an exception; it doesn't support the old style of join).

The SQL-89 style supports only inner joins. To support outer joins, some vendors, such as Oracle and Microsoft, invented nonstandard syntax (which will not be shown in this book). The proprietary syntax is no longer needed because Oracle and Microsoft SQL have supported the SQL-92 join syntax for many years.

Oracle supports SQL-92 join syntax since Oracle 9i (circa 2001).

Microsoft supports SQL-92 join syntax since SQL Server 7.0 (circa 1998). Microsoft even removed support for its proprietary outer join syntax in SQL Server 2012.

It's recommended to use the SQL-92 style for all joins. There's no advantage to using the old style, and your code will be more recognizable by programmers who are familiar with standard syntax if you use the SQL-92 style for both inner joins and outer joins.

Mini-Antipattern: NATURAL JOIN

The syntax for JOIN includes optional shorthand NATURAL JOIN. With this form, you don't specify the conditions for the join because they are defined implicitly. In a natural join, all columns that have the same name in both tables are used for the join condition. Also, the comparison operator is always equals (=).

The following three queries do the same join, assuming both tables have columns named Col1 and Col2, and no other columns in common.

```
SELECT ... FROM Table1 NATURAL JOIN Table2;

SELECT ... FROM Table1 JOIN Table2 USING (Col1, Col2);

SELECT ... FROM Table1 JOIN Table2
    ON Table1.Col1 = Table2.Col1 AND Table1.Col2 = Table2.Col2;
```

This has confused many software developers. Since this form of join is called *natural*, and things that are natural are generally good, should we use NATURAL JOIN more often?

In popular use, SQL tables may include columns of the same name, without being used for joins.

For example, a convention in modern applications is that each table uses a serially incrementing integer column for its primary key, and this column is named id in every table. But the integers of one table increment independently from the integers of all other tables. A row with id=1234 in one table doesn't reference the row with id=1234 of another table, unless the tables are in a one-to-one relationship.

Some applications also use a convention to add timestamp columns created_at and updated_at in every table, to track changes. It would be very unlikely that you'd want to join one table to another where these timestamps are equal, but that's what NATURAL JOIN would do.

If you use NATURAL JOIN, you must name columns carefully in all your tables. Don't reuse names unless the columns are supposed to be used for joins. If you don't enforce this naming policy, then your join queries might return unexpected results.

It's easier and safer to adopt a code standard to avoid using NATURAL JOIN. Use one of the other two syntax forms, naming the columns in the join condition explicitly—either with USING, or else by fully writing out the join conditions.

You seldom, if ever, see NATURAL JOIN used in real projects, and this is natural.

He who follows two hares is sure to catch neither.

David Evans MacDonnel

CHAPTER 3

Relational Division

I visited a startup company in San Francisco to help them with their database design. Their main business concept was a photo-sharing site, but there are already plenty of similar startups. Their distinct business value was to allow a collection of photos to be organized by applying labels for location, time, type of photo, people who appear in it, and so on. For example, a set of labels might be `[Lake Tahoe, Afternoon, Action, George, Julia]`.

Once the photos were labeled, the user could search their photos by any combination of labels.

The problem was that the founders of the startup had the concept of their business value, but they had no idea how to design a database to make these queries both flexible and optimized. They wanted me to show them how to create an SQL index to support such queries. This was years before vector search features became popular, so they were limited to common B-tree indexes.

B-tree indexes can be defined for multiple columns, but you must search by columns starting with the first column of the index, and skip no columns.

How were we going to make a system that allowed users to define flexible search criteria based on their choice of multiple labels?

Objective: Matching a List of Values

In the Visage application, suppose users can write posts and posts can be assigned one or more tags, to put them in categories. There is a many-to-many relationship between posts and tags.

You can imagine that a common type of SQL query is to search for posts that have any one of a list of tags. These can be found using either of the queries at the top of the next page.

Division/anti/or-list.sql

```
SELECT post_id FROM post_tag
WHERE tag_id IN (1, 2, 3);

SELECT post_id FROM post_tag
WHERE tag_id = 1 OR tag_id = 2 OR tag_id = 3;
```

Now, suppose you want only posts that match *all* of a specific list of tags.

For that search, you would need something complementary to the IN() predicate, but matching all values, as though the terms in the WHERE clause were combined with AND instead of OR. This seems like it's a common enough query that SQL should do what you want, but there's a problem, as you'll see in the next section.

Antipattern: Searching Multiple Rows in a WHERE Clause

The mistake is to try to write a condition in the WHERE clause to compare one column to several values and expect all of the comparisons to be satisfied.

Division/anti/and-list.sql

```
SELECT post_id FROM post_tag
WHERE tag_id = 1 AND tag_id = 2 AND tag_id = 3;
```

This doesn't work. It's not a syntax error, but it's a logic error. It always returns an empty result, even if you know that some posts exist with all of the tags you list.

The reason is that expressions in a WHERE clause only apply to one row at a time. On a given row, at most one of the values might match. There is no row where the tag_id is all three values simultaneously. Therefore, the WHERE expression is bound to be false on every row.

How to Recognize the Antipattern

- "Is there a way in SQL to search like the IN() predicate, but for multiple AND terms instead of multiple OR terms?"

  No, SQL doesn't have an easy predicate to test this because it would require comparing multiple rows, unlike other predicates you can use in a WHERE clause.

- "Why is my query result empty? I have a list of values, and I want rows that match all the values in the list."

  The query probably tried to compare a column to multiple different values, which can't match any row.

- "I store data in an Entity-Attribute-Value table, and I want to find entities that have specific values in multiple attributes."

  This is one of the common difficulties of the EAV solution.

Legitimate Uses of the Antipattern

Although it's normal for every antipattern to be used in some exceptional cases where there isn't another solution, in this rare case, there really isn't a legitimate use for this antipattern.

There are many legitimate cases of needing *sets* of rows that match multiple values, such as the search for tags that you saw in the previous examples. Or searching for occurrences of an event in every week or every year. Or making sure every member of a group of users has taken an action. Or verifying that all mandatory fields of a data entry form have been filled in.

But the mistake of trying to compare a column to multiple values in a WHERE clause is never going to work. This is based on a misunderstanding of how SQL predicates work.

Solution: Using Relational Division

There is a solution. This type of search is called *relational division*.

This operation is used less frequently than other relational operations like JOIN or UNION. SQL has a keyword JOIN to make joins convenient, but no keyword exists for relational division. The solutions for relational division must be implemented using other SQL syntax.

Why Is It Called Relational Division?

The name comes from relational algebra. A cross join in relational algebra is analogous to multiplication because the result of joining one set of N rows to another set of M rows is a new set with $N \times M$ rows. In fact, the symbol for a cross join is the traditional multiplication symbol, ×.

Like in arithmetic or other algebras, the multiplication operation has an inverse operation, which is called *division*. In arithmetic, division is: *dividend* ÷ *divisor* = *quotient*. The operation can be reversed: *quotient* × *divisor* = *dividend*.

A similar algebra works for relational operations. Relationally divide the dividend table by the divisor table, and the result is the quotient table. This can be reversed, too: cross-join the quotient table with the divisor table, and you get the dividend table.

The following sections show several solutions for relational division in SQL.

Self-Join Solution

As you saw in Chapter 2, Fear of JOINs, on page 11, if you need an expression in the WHERE clause to apply to multiple rows, you can join multiple rows from different table references to make a new row with all the columns side-by-side.

"post_tag"

post_id	tag_id	
123	1	t1
123	2	t2
123	3	t3

t1 JOIN t2 JOIN t3

t1.post_id	t1.tag_id	t2.post_id	t2.tag_id	t3.post_id	t3.tag_id
123	1	123	2	123	3

This join happens before the rows are evaluated by conditions in the WHERE clause, so you can write an expression in a WHERE clause that references all of the columns of the joined row, which originally came from different rows. The following query shows how to do this with a self-join.

Division/soln/self-join.sql

```
SELECT post_id
FROM post_tag AS t1
INNER JOIN post_tag AS t2 USING (post_id)
INNER JOIN post_tag AS t3 USING (post_id)
WHERE t1.tag_id = 1 AND t2.tag_id = 2 AND t3.tag_id = 3;
```

An inner join requires that a row exists on both sides of each join. So, if any of the rows don't exist, the join has no match, and the join produces an empty result. If there is a third join or any further joins, they can't match against an empty result, so they also produce an empty result. This means a row must exist that satisfies every condition, or else the whole query produces an empty result.

The preceding example shows a relational division search for a set of three values. The solution using JOIN requires one table reference for each of these three values. If you need to search for posts matching four values or five values, then you need to join to more table references. This means a single query can't be reused to match any arbitrary set of values. To make this solution more general-purpose, you need to use client code to format a query with a variable number of joins, based on the set of values you search for.

The following Python script shows one example of code that generates a custom SQL query depending on the number of values in an array:

Division/soln/self-join-dynamic.py

```
import psycopg2

conn = psycopg2.connect("dbname='visage' host='localhost'")

desired_tags = [1, 2, 3]

with conn.cursor() as cur:
    using = ''
    join_terms = []
    where_terms = []
    for i, tag in enumerate(desired_tags, start=1):
        join_terms.append(f"post_tag AS t{i} {using}")
        using = "USING (post_id)"
        where_terms.append(f"t{i}.tag_id = %s")
    sql = f"""
        SELECT post_id
        FROM {" INNER JOIN ".join(join_terms)}
        WHERE {" AND ".join(where_terms)}
    """
    cur.execute(sql, desired_tags)
    print(cur.fetchall())
```

Note that the Python function for imploding an array is coincidentally also named join(). This is unrelated to the SQL operation to join tables.

The join solution might become impractical if the set of values is too large. Some implementations of SQL have a fixed limit on the number of joins in a query. For example, MySQL has a hard limit of 61 table references in a query.

Aggregation Solution

A relational division query is searching for a set of rows that satisfy the condition. SQL has a general method for filtering groups of rows after they are aggregated, by using GROUP BY and HAVING. This solution uses no joins.

Division/soln/having-count-strict.sql

```
SELECT post_id
FROM post_tag
GROUP BY post_id
HAVING COUNT(tag_id) = 3;
```

As you saw earlier, a WHERE clause applies to individual rows, whereas the HAVING clause applies after SQL has grouped the rows, so HAVING applies a condition to the group.

Look at the rows of data in the following figure.

"post_tag"

post_id	tag_id	
123	1	
123	2	group with the desired tags
123	3	
456	1	group missing a desired tag
456	3	
789	1	
789	2	group with extra tags
789	3	
789	5	

The first group includes tag_id values 1, 2, and 3, and there are exactly three distinct values of tag_id in that group. Therefore, the COUNT(tag_id) is three, and the group satisfies the condition.

The second group has only two tags, so it can't satisfy the condition.

The third group has an extra tag. You might want this group to fail the condition, since it doesn't have *exactly* the three tags you named. Alternatively, you might want the group to pass because the group has *at least* the three tags you named. You can count only rows for tags that are one of the three desired tags, using a condition in the WHERE clause.

Division/soln/having-count-nonstrict.sql

```
SELECT post_id
FROM post_tag
WHERE tag_id IN (1, 2, 3)
GROUP BY post_id
HAVING COUNT(tag_id) = 3;
```

The WHERE clause filters only rows that match one of the values in the list, so any extra tag_id values are ignored. Then, the rows are grouped, so an aggregate function like COUNT() only considers the subset of rows for each value of post_id.

If the post_tag table were defined with a different primary key that doesn't ensure each pair of (post_id, tag_id) is unique, then we would use COUNT(DISTINCT tag_id) instead of COUNT(tag_id) because we want to find posts that have three different tag values, not one of the tags repeated three times.

Here is another solution that uses aggregation to make a string of the list of tag_id values found, and then compares that to a string that is the desired list. There are two variations. The first is strict, in that the tags must match the list of three exactly. If the post has other tags besides those, the aggregated string won't be exactly '1,2,3' and the condition won't be satisfied.

Division/soln/having-string-strict.sql

```
SELECT post_id
FROM post_tag
GROUP BY post_id
HAVING STRING_AGG(tag_id::character varying, ',' ORDER BY tag_id) = '1,2,3';
```

The second variation is less strict because it has a WHERE clause that filters out any tag_id's besides the three you're interested in. Even if a given post has some additional tags, those are excluded before the group is defined, and the aggregated string matches the one in the condition exactly.

Division/soln/having-string-nonstrict.sql

```
SELECT post_id
FROM post_tag
WHERE tag_id IN (1, 2, 3)
GROUP BY post_id
HAVING STRING_AGG(tag_id::character varying, ',' ORDER BY tag_id) = '1,2,3';
```

To extend this solution to match larger sets of values, you need to modify the HAVING clause to compare to a larger count or a longer list of comma-separated values. That's easy enough to make dynamic because those are simply scalar values. However, if you also need the query to have a condition in the WHERE clause so other values are ignored, then format the query with a variable-length IN() predicate.

Division/soln/having-count-dynamic.py

```
import psycopg2

conn = psycopg2.connect("dbname='visage' host='localhost'")

desired_tags = [1, 2, 3]

with conn.cursor() as cur:
    sql = f"""
        SELECT post_id
        FROM post_tag
        WHERE tag_id IN ({','.join(['%s'] * len(desired_tags))})
        GROUP BY post_id
        HAVING COUNT(tag_id) = {len(desired_tags)};
    """
    cur.execute(sql, desired_tags)
    print(cur.fetchall())
```

It's not unusual to use application code to format an SQL query as a string when you need the query to include variable terms. Do continue to use query parameters instead of appending untrusted values into the query.

Not Exists Solution

This solution uses neither joins nor aggregation. If you really want to develop SQL solutions by adopting a set-oriented perspective, this is a good example.

Think of your three desired tags as a set itself. Reference this set of data in your query by storing it in a temporary table or a common table expression.

The idea is to search the post_tag table for those cases where one of the desired tags is not found, and then return the complement of that set.

Division/soln/not-exists.sql

```
WITH desired_tag(tag_id) AS (
  VALUES (1), (2), (3)
)
SELECT DISTINCT post_id
FROM post_tag p1
WHERE NOT EXISTS (
  SELECT * FROM desired_tag d
  WHERE NOT EXISTS (
    SELECT * FROM post_tag p2
    WHERE p1.post_id = p2.post_id
      AND p2.tag_id = d.tag_id
  )
);
```

In the preceding example, the innermost subquery searches for any of the desired tags that are not present in post_tag. The middle subquery searches for cases where a given post_id has no such "missing" tag.

Extending this solution to match larger sets of values is easier if you first load your desired values into a temporary table.

Choosing a Solution

You've seen several examples of solutions for relational division queries in this chapter. Which one is the best? How can you choose?

The answer is, it depends on the implementation of SQL in the RDBMS product you use. It may also depend on the performance characteristics of your server platform. For example, if temporary tables are costly to create, then a join solution may be faster. What works best for some other project isn't necessarily what will work best for your project.

The best way to identify the best solution—given your data on your server with your RDBMS version—is to test several solutions in that environment, and compare their results and performance. For smaller applications, the difference may be so small that it's not worth optimizing, and it's worth choosing the simplest solution that works. For applications that have high scale and where finding every optimization is important enough that it justifies extra testing, then it's up to you to invest that time.

A language like SQL is designed to streamline the most common tasks. For the uncommon tasks, expect to do a little more work.

Mini-Antipattern: Aggregation Functions in the WHERE Clause

As described earlier in this chapter, the expression in a WHERE clause applies only to one row at a time. If you have a condition that applies to a group of rows, it makes no sense to put that in a WHERE clause of the query reading those rows.

For example, suppose your task is to return posts that have more than three tags. You try the following query, but it returns an error:

```
SELECT post_id
FROM post_tag
WHERE COUNT(*) > 3
GROUP BY post_id;
```

```
ERROR:  aggregate functions are not allowed in WHERE
LINE 3: WHERE COUNT(*) > 3
              ^
```

You can use the HAVING clause to restrict the result based on aggregates:

```
SELECT post_id
FROM post_tag
GROUP BY post_id
HAVING COUNT(*) > 3;
```

Alternatively, you can run a subquery that performs grouping. The subquery returns one row per group. Apply a condition on these rows in the WHERE clause of the outer query:

```
SELECT post_id
FROM (
  SELECT post_id, COUNT(*) AS count
  FROM post_tag
  GROUP BY post_id
) AS t
WHERE count > 3;
```

You can reference the name of an alias—in this case, for an aggregate expression—in the WHERE clause only if the alias is defined in a subquery.

Give me a place to stand and with a lever I will move the world.

Archimedes of Syracuse

CHAPTER 4

Dynamic Pivot

Your manager, Paul, sends you a request. "We need a report of traffic on the site. Please display the total comments by month, in columns. And make it data-driven, so the report automatically includes future months as they get traffic."

You know how to write a query that gives subtotals using `COUNT()` and `GROUP BY`, but that outputs in rows, not columns. How can you turn that result on its side, with output in columns like a spreadsheet? And how can you meet your boss's requirement that the report expand to handle future months?

Objective: Turning the Table

It's a natural request to display the results of a query in a tabular format, using as many columns as needed to make it easy to read. Effective presentation is important.

SQL query results are like the result of a function; they are raw data, which isn't necessarily the most readable format. But you still have to present the data in the format your boss requested. They want a column for each month, and they want the report to include new columns for future months:

2022-01	2022-02	2022-03	...	2024-12	2025-01	2025-02
1234576	2048327	6060842		8675309	11041357	12345678

This type of query is called a *pivot table query* or a *crosstab query*.

Antipattern: Using a Single Query

To produce the report format your boss requested, the temptation is to develop a single query that populates "dynamic" columns (that is, additional columns are appended to the result as the query discovers new data). This is where you get stuck searching for a solution. Nothing you try as a single query works.

Wildcard in the Select-List

You know that you can use the wildcard * in an SQL select-list to populate a variable number of columns. This may sound like it's on the right track, but it doesn't work to add columns for each distinct value examined. The wildcard is only a shorthand for a fixed set of columns, corresponding to the columns in tables referenced in the FROM clause.

You might try to use GROUP BY, thinking that it would produce a value for each year and month. But GROUP BY doesn't do what you want.

Pivot/anti/group-by.sql

```
SELECT *
FROM comment
GROUP BY TO_CHAR(created_at, 'YYYY-MM');

SELECT comment_id, comment_text, in_reply_to, user_id, created_at
FROM comment
GROUP BY TO_CHAR(created_at, 'YYYY-MM');
```

In fact, both forms of this query result in an error:

```
ERROR:  column "comment.comment_id" must appear in the GROUP BY clause
or be used in an aggregate function
LINE 1: SELECT comment_id, comment_text, in_reply_to, user_id, creat...
               ^
```

A query with GROUP BY would produce an additional *row* for each distinct value resulting from the grouping expression, not an additional column. Besides that, the values in the rest of the columns become ambiguous, and that's the reason for the error. See the chapter "Ambiguous Groups" in *SQL Antipatterns Volume 1 [Kar22]* for more explanation.

Correlated Subqueries in the Select-List

You can use subqueries in a select-list, such that each subquery has a monthly subtotal. This produces the result you want if you specify a column for each range of dates. This means you need to know the dates present in the table before you write the query. There's no way to make it expand the list of these expressions automatically as time goes on and traffic occurs in additional months. You'll have to change the query to add a new column every time the next month of traffic is added to the table.

Pivot/anti/subquery.sql

```
SELECT
  (SELECT COUNT(*) FROM comment
   WHERE created_at BETWEEN '2022-01-01' AND '2022-02-01') AS "2022-01",
  (SELECT COUNT(*) FROM comment
   WHERE created_at BETWEEN '2022-02-01' AND '2022-03-01') AS "2022-02",
```

```
(SELECT COUNT(*) FROM comment
 WHERE created_at BETWEEN '2022-03-01' AND '2022-04-01') AS "2022-03",
-- ...
(SELECT COUNT(*) FROM comment
 WHERE created_at BETWEEN '2024-12-01' AND '2025-01-01') AS "2024-12",
(SELECT COUNT(*) FROM comment
 WHERE created_at BETWEEN '2025-01-01' AND '2025-02-01') AS "2025-01",
(SELECT COUNT(*) FROM comment
 WHERE created_at BETWEEN '2025-02-01' AND '2025-03-01') AS "2025-02";
```

Correlated subqueries in the select-list have a high cost with respect to performance because most SQL implementations repeat the execution for each subquery.

Conditional Aggregation

Instead of using subqueries, you can use an aggregation function like COUNT(), applied to a subset of rows. This is called *conditional aggregation*. Functions like COUNT() ignore rows where the expression inside the function is NULL. If you use an expression as an argument to COUNT() that evaluates to a non-NULL value on certain rows, and NULL otherwise, then it counts the subset of rows where the expression is non-NULL.

Pivot/anti/conditional-agg.sql

```
SELECT
  COUNT(CASE WHEN created_at BETWEEN '2022-01-01' AND '2022-02-01'
    THEN 1 ELSE NULL END) AS "2022-01",
  COUNT(CASE WHEN created_at BETWEEN '2022-02-01' AND '2022-03-01'
    THEN 1 ELSE NULL END) AS "2022-02",
  COUNT(CASE WHEN created_at BETWEEN '2022-03-01' AND '2022-04-01'
    THEN 1 ELSE NULL END) AS "2022-03",
  -- ...
  COUNT(CASE WHEN created_at BETWEEN '2024-12-01' AND '2025-01-01'
    THEN 1 ELSE NULL END) AS "2024-12",
  COUNT(CASE WHEN created_at BETWEEN '2025-01-01' AND '2025-02-01'
    THEN 1 ELSE NULL END) AS "2025-01",
  COUNT(CASE WHEN created_at BETWEEN '2025-02-01' AND '2025-03-01'
    THEN 1 ELSE NULL END) AS "2025-02"
FROM comment;
```

This also requires you to spell out each column explicitly. There's no syntax to make the select-list populate more columns than those you specify.

If you are using PostgreSQL or SQLite, the FILTER clause (introduced in SQL:2003) assists conditional aggregation. This does the same thing as the previous example, but you may find it makes the code more clear. There's an example at the top of the next page.

Pivot/anti/filter.sql

```
SELECT
  COUNT(*) FILTER (WHERE created_at
    BETWEEN '2022-01-01' AND '2022-02-01') AS "2022-01",
  COUNT(*) FILTER (WHERE created_at
    BETWEEN '2022-02-01' AND '2022-03-01') AS "2022-02",
  COUNT(*) FILTER (WHERE created_at
    BETWEEN '2022-03-01' AND '2022-04-01') AS "2022-03",
  -- ...
  COUNT(*) FILTER (WHERE created_at
    BETWEEN '2024-12-01' AND '2025-01-01') AS "2024-12",
  COUNT(*) FILTER (WHERE created_at
    BETWEEN '2025-01-01' AND '2025-02-01') AS "2025-01",
  COUNT(*) FILTER (WHERE created_at
    BETWEEN '2025-02-01' AND '2025-03-01') AS "2025-02"
FROM comment;
```

As of this writing, SQL products that implement the FILTER clause include DuckDB 1.4.0, Oracle 23.26.1, PostgreSQL 18, and SQLite 3.51.0. Other brands may implement it in the future.

Vendor-Specific Solutions

This section is about nonstandard, proprietary solutions implemented by some SQL vendors. Proprietary solutions are not in the SQL standard, so they are less likely to be adopted by other SQL products. In some cases, a proprietary feature may even be deprecated by the vendor who implemented it if a similar standard solution becomes mainstream.

PostgreSQL developed a CROSSTAB() function to help programmers write queries that map rows to columns. The crosstab is not truly dynamic because you must still specify the columns. The following query shows how you can use the CROSSTAB() function for the example of reporting comments per month:

Pivot/anti/postgresql-crosstab.sql

```
-- Enable the tablefunc extension before using CROSSTAB().
CREATE EXTENSION IF NOT EXISTS tablefunc;

SELECT * FROM CROSSTAB(
  'SELECT NULL, TO_CHAR(created_at, ''YYYY-MM''), COUNT(*) FROM comment
  GROUP BY TO_CHAR(created_at, ''YYYY-MM'') ORDER BY 2'
) AS ct(row_name TEXT,
  "2022-01" BIGINT, "2022-02" BIGINT, "2022-03" BIGINT, -- ...
  "2024-12" BIGINT, "2025-01" BIGINT, "2025-02" BIGINT);
```

Several other brands of RDBMS, including Microsoft SQL Server, Oracle, and Snowflake, use a PIVOT keyword. Each brand has implemented it differently.

Pivot/anti/microsoft-pivot.sql

```
SELECT 'Count' AS CommentsPerMonth,
  [2022-01], [2022-02], [2022-03], [2024-12], [2025-01], [2025-02]
FROM (
  SELECT FORMAT([created_at], 'yyyy-MM') AS ym, comment_id
  FROM comment
) AS SourceTable
PIVOT (
  COUNT(comment_id) FOR ym IN
  ([2022-01], [2022-02], [2022-03], [2024-12], [2025-01], [2025-02])
) AS PivotTable;
```

None of the solutions in this antipattern section accomplishes the goal of accommodating new data dynamically, except Snowflake's implementation of PIVOT or Oracle's implementation of PIVOT XML.

How to Recognize the Antipattern

- "How can I write a query that returns a dynamic number of columns, one for each value?"

  This question may be asked in different ways, but the answer is always the same—aside from the use of wildcards, SQL cannot return a dynamic set of columns.

Legitimate Uses of the Antipattern

You can use a workaround to simulate a dynamic set of columns by running a query that returns a single column, which formats a dynamic set of values as a JSON document:

Pivot/soln/json-objectagg.sql

```
SELECT JSONB_OBJECT_AGG(ym, count)
FROM (
  SELECT TO_CHAR(created_at, 'YYYY-MM'), COUNT(*)
  FROM comment
  GROUP BY TO_CHAR(created_at, 'YYYY-MM')
) AS t(ym, count);
```

The result of the preceding query is a single JSON column with the year-month strings as object keys and the counts as object values:

```
{
  "2022-01" : 1234576, "2022-02" : 2048327, "2022-03" : 6060842, ...
  "2024-12" : 8675309, "2025-01" : 11041357, "2025-02": 12345678
}
```

Your client application fetches this as a single string, not as individual columns of a query result. To separate the JSON object into a data structure that the client application can use, explode the string. For example, in Python, you could use json.loads() to convert a string containing JSON into a dict.

Solution: Using Code to Assist

The most important fact to keep in mind is that in a given query, the columns in the select-list are fixed; you can't make a query that extends its own columns dynamically.

There are solutions to solve this task, using a little bit of code to help out.

Run Two Queries

The pivot query needs to have an expression for each column, which means you need to know how many columns the query should return, given the data currently in your table.

You can answer this by running another query first:

Pivot/soln/distinct-months.sql

```
SELECT DISTINCT TO_CHAR(created_at, 'YYYY-MM') AS ym
FROM comment;
```

The result of this query consists of the set of year-month values corresponding exactly to the columns you need in your pivot query. You can write a loop with code to add an SQL expression for each of these values, and append these to a string that is the pivot query that handles the current data.

You can choose which style of pivot query you want to build.

The style with conditional aggregation expressions:

Pivot/soln/dynamic-conditional-agg.py

```
import psycopg2
import psycopg2.extras

conn = psycopg2.connect("dbname='visage' host='localhost'")

with conn.cursor(cursor_factory=psycopg2.extras.RealDictCursor) as cur:
    sql = """
        SELECT DISTINCT TO_CHAR(created_at, 'YYYY-MM') AS ym FROM comment
    """
    cur.execute(sql)
    ym_list = cur.fetchall()

    pivot_exprs = [f"""
        COUNT(CASE TO_CHAR(created_at, 'YYYY-MM')
            WHEN '{ym['ym']}' THEN 1 END) AS "{ym['ym']}"
    """ for ym in ym_list]

    sql = f"""
        SELECT {','.join(pivot_exprs)} FROM comment
```

```
    """
    cur.execute(sql)
    print(cur.fetchall())
```

The style with subqueries:

Pivot/soln/dynamic-subqueries.py

```
import psycopg2
import psycopg2.extras

conn = psycopg2.connect("dbname='visage' host='localhost'")

with conn.cursor(cursor_factory=psycopg2.extras.RealDictCursor) as cur:
    sql = """
        SELECT DISTINCT TO_CHAR(created_at, 'YYYY-MM') AS ym,
          DATE_TRUNC('month', created_at)::date AS start,
          DATE_TRUNC('month', created_at)::date
          + MAKE_INTERVAL(MONTHS=>1) AS end
        FROM comment
    """
    cur.execute(sql)
    ym_list = cur.fetchall()

    pivot_exprs = [f"""
        (SELECT COUNT(*) FROM comment
         WHERE created_at BETWEEN
            '{ym['start']}' AND '{ym['end']}') AS "{ym['ym']}"
    """ for ym in ym_list]

    sql = f"""
        SELECT {','.join(pivot_exprs)}
    """
    cur.execute(sql)
    print(cur.fetchall())
```

The query that uses PostgreSQL's CROSSTAB() function:

Pivot/soln/dynamic-crosstab.py

```
import psycopg2
import psycopg2.extras

conn = psycopg2.connect("dbname='visage' host='localhost'")

with conn.cursor(cursor_factory=psycopg2.extras.RealDictCursor) as cur:
    sql = """
        SELECT DISTINCT TO_CHAR(created_at, 'YYYY-MM') AS ym FROM comment
    """
    cur.execute(sql)
    ym_list = cur.fetchall()

    crosstab_columns = [f"""
        "{ym['ym']}" BIGINT
    """ for ym in ym_list]

    sql = f"""
```

```
        SELECT * FROM CROSSTAB(
          'SELECT NULL, TO_CHAR(created_at, ''YYYY-MM''), COUNT(*)
          FROM comment
          GROUP BY TO_CHAR(created_at, ''YYYY-MM'') ORDER BY 2'
        ) AS ct(row_name TEXT,
          {','.join(crosstab_columns)})
    """
    cur.execute(sql)
    print(cur.fetchall())
```

In each case, the preceding Python examples show code that converts the list of distinct dates into expressions or subqueries needed to populate the columns of the pivot query. In Python, the list comprehension syntax is a concise way of looping over the dates.

Post-Processing with Client Code

An alternative solution is to run one query that returns rows instead of columns. This handles any range of dates currently represented in the data. You then write code to fetch the results and manipulate them to present in the pivoted manner.

Pivot/soln/post-process.py

```
import psycopg2
import psycopg2.extras

conn = psycopg2.connect("dbname='visage' host='localhost'")

with conn.cursor(cursor_factory=psycopg2.extras.RealDictCursor) as cur:
    sql = """
        SELECT TO_CHAR(created_at, 'YYYY-MM') AS ym, COUNT(*) AS count
        FROM comment
        GROUP BY TO_CHAR(created_at, 'YYYY-MM')
    """
    cur.execute(sql)

    pivoted_row = {}
    for row in cur:
        pivoted_row[row['ym']] = row['count']

    print(pivoted_row)
```

In the preceding Python example, the results are copied to a dict, with the YYYY-MM label as the key and the respective count as the value. This dict has as many keys as rows returned by the SQL query, so it has pivoted the results from rows into "columns."

One way or the other, you need to write some code to support this query.

Mini-Antipattern: Operand Must Contain One Column

What does the following error mean?

```
# SELECT * FROM post_tag WHERE post_id = (123, 2);
ERROR:  operator does not exist: bigint = record
```

In MySQL, the error is different, but even less clear:

```
mysql> SELECT * FROM post_tag WHERE post_id = (123, 2);
ERROR 1241 (21000): Operand should contain 1 column(s)
```

A *scalar* is a single value, like a number, a string, a reference to a scalar column, or an expression that results in a scalar. A *record* is a list of scalar values.

These preceding errors mean that the SQL queries are comparing an integer scalar to a record with the = operator.

It's possible to compare a record to another record. The syntax is a list of scalars, delimited by parentheses. For example, you can compare two records as a shorthand for comparing each of the scalar values as terms of an AND expression:

```
SELECT * FROM post_tag WHERE (post_id, tag_id) = (123, 2);
```

The records are equal if every element in one record is equal to the element in the same position in the other record. This requires the records to have the same number of elements. If the records don't have the same length, then they aren't simply unequal. It's an error to compare them at all.

The apples-to-oranges nature of comparing scalars to records also comes up during searches using subqueries. If the subquery returns more than one column, this means it returns records and can only be compared to a record in the outer query. If your query compares the subquery result to a scalar, then the subquery cannot return multiple columns.

PostgreSQL:

```
# SELECT * FROM post_tag WHERE post_id IN (SELECT * FROM post);
ERROR:  subquery has too many columns
```

MySQL:

```
mysql> SELECT * FROM post_tag WHERE post_id IN (SELECT * FROM post);
ERROR 1241 (21000): Operand should contain 1 column(s)
```

Another case for the error is when returning results.

MySQL can use records in comparisons, but it doesn't have a data type for a record. It can't store a record as the value of a column in a table or as part of a query result set. This means if your query has parentheses around the select-list, it looks like you meant to return a single column consisting of a record.

```
mysql> SELECT (post_id, tag_id) FROM post_tag;
ERROR 1241 (21000): Operand should contain 1 column(s)
```

MySQL gives an error, complaining that the "operand," that is, one of the expressions in the select-list, looks like a record. MySQL only supports scalar expressions in the select-list.

In contrast, PostgreSQL has a data type called `record`, so it allows you to return a record:

```
# SELECT (post_id, tag_id) FROM post_tag;
   row
---------
 (123,1)
 (123,2)
 (123,3)
 ...
```

Be careful to match the size of a record to its context. Don't compare a record to another record of a different size, and don't use a record where a scalar is required.

"Begin at the beginning," the King said, very gravely, "and go on till you come to the end: then stop."

Lewis Carroll

CHAPTER 5

Pagination: Take It from the Top

"We got another incident report from a user about performance when viewing the Visage daily," Chetana, the customer support representative, announces to the meeting. The *daily* is a view of comments the user subscribes to. It's the most commonly viewed screen in the application.

The product manager, Terry, frowns and turns to Cleo, the software engineer. "I thought we resolved that."

Cleo nods her head confidently. "We have tests specifically for performance," she says. "We can't reproduce a performance issue."

"One new detail," Chetana adds. "This user says the performance is okay when they view the first page of the daily, but it gets slower the longer they read."

"You mean they move to the second page and further, and the performance gets worse?" Terry asks.

"Yeah, and we contacted the other users who reported issues last week," Chetana continues. "And they confirm that the same thing happens for them. The performance degrades as they advance to further pages."

Cleo's eyes grow wide. "Our performance test only uses simulated daily content with a single page," she admits softly.

Objective: Presenting Query Results in Pages

It's common for a software application to present data using *pagination*. This means that if the result set of a query is too long, only an initial subset of it is shown at first. It might not even be the result the user intended to query, and there's no reason to overwhelm them or their browser window with a result of unlimited size. Especially if the result might be thousands of rows, or even larger. Who would want to look at that?

The view typically shows a fixed-size subset of rows, with a user interface control to request the following subset. The user can choose to click that control if the result is what they requested and they want to read more.

The objective is to present data that is the result of an SQL query, showing successive subsets, and make it quick to advance to the next subset. This turns out to be a little more tricky than it sounds.

Antipattern: Mistaking Offset for Optimization

Each brand of SQL database has some form of syntax to support paginated queries. PostgreSQL, MySQL, and SQLite have an optional clause LIMIT with OFFSET. The following example shows a query that skips past the first subset of five rows and shows the second five rows. If there are fewer than five rows in the second page, the query returns as many as it finds.

Pagination/anti/limit-offset.sql
```
SELECT *
FROM comment
ORDER BY comment_id
LIMIT 5 OFFSET 5;
```

Standard SQL:2008 introduced a slightly different syntax to do the same thing. This is supported in some SQL products, for example, starting in PostgreSQL 8.4, Oracle 12, Microsoft SQL Server 2012, and IBM DB2 8, but not yet in MySQL or SQLite.

Pagination/anti/fetch-next.sql
```
SELECT *
FROM comment
ORDER BY comment_id
OFFSET 5
FETCH NEXT 5 ROWS ONLY;
```

Both of these styles implement pagination if you keep the number of rows in the LIMIT or FETCH clauses fixed at the number of rows in your desired page, and increment the OFFSET clause by multiples of that number.

The query returns the result you want, but the problem is that as you advance through the pages, it gets slower and slower, even if you have added an index to your table.

An index helps to search for a row or a range of rows that contain a specific value. Queries with OFFSET search by row position, not by value.

If you could assume that primary key values are effectively row numbers—integers starting at 1 and not missing any values—then you could query using a range query instead of using OFFSET.

Pagination/anti/range.sql
```
SELECT *
FROM comment
WHERE comment_id BETWEEN 6 AND 10;
```

But the query engine can't assume that a row in the *Nth* position is guaranteed to contain the value *N* that corresponds to its row number, so it can't use the index to look up that row. Anyone could have spoiled the consecutive values by inserting a new row or deleting a row.

Besides that, a query could have a WHERE clause, so it doesn't return every row in the table, or it could use a JOIN to another table, so the result may have multiple rows for each respective primary key value in the first table.

For these reasons, the only reliable way for a query engine to implement OFFSET is to count the rows in that query result at the time it is executed. This means it must examine the rows that will be skipped in the result, according to the OFFSET requested, plus the last rows included in the requested set.

In the following figure, the dark grey rows represent rows of the table you want your pagination query to return. The light grey rows are skipped and are not returned in the query result, but the SQL engine must still examine these rows. The bar to the left of each set of rows shows how many rows are examined in total.

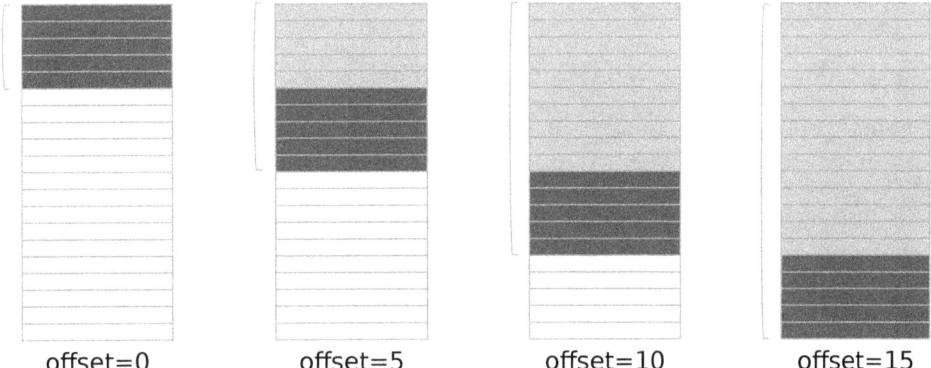

As your query requests pages with higher values for OFFSET, the number of examined rows in each query execution grows larger and larger.

The number of rows examined by a query has a direct effect on the performance you perceive.

How to Recognize the Antipattern

- "Help! The queries keep getting slower as I advance through the pages of a paginated result!"

  This shows that it's expensive for the query to locate pages by position because it has to examine all preceding rows on the way.

- "I added an index, and I even used an optimizer hint to force the query to use the index. Why doesn't it help to find the 2995590th row?"

  Indexes help to optimize lookup by value, not by position.

- "How do I show page numbers and give a link to allow the user to choose a page to view, if I don't know the last page?"

  Notice that many search engines don't have this feature. They may link to the next page, and the first few numbered pages, but not the last page.

  Beware of creating an interface that allows web-crawling bots to page through your entire database—because some will.

- "Why are rows sometimes repeated when I view the next page? Sometimes rows even vanish, as if they fall in between pages!"

  Using `LIMIT` and `OFFSET` counts the position of rows in the current query, without regard to which rows appeared on the last page you viewed. If anyone inserted or deleted rows, this changes the position of all subsequent rows.

Legitimate Uses of the Antipattern

Pagination itself isn't an antipattern. Many applications are required to show query results in this way.

The antipattern is using pagination queries and expecting them to be efficient, even with arbitrarily large offsets.

There are some queries that can't be optimized, as you'll see in the next section. In that case, you have to use `OFFSET` and bear the cost of an inefficient operation.

Solution: Changing the Rules

Your query can't avoid examining the rows omitted from the result by OFFSET. This means it's hard to optimize a pagination query that skips rows. But a query that uses LIMIT or FETCH does have an advantage: once the SQL engine reads enough rows to satisfy the number of rows requested, the result is returned, and no more rows are examined. If you could make a query that examines only rows in the page you want, instead of all the preceding rows, that would optimize the query.

Keyset Pagination

One way to do this is to use a range query with an inequality that starts at the first row of a page and includes all subsequent rows. Using LIMIT or FETCH, it would stop examining rows as soon as possible.

The following query reads the rows that follow a specific comment_id, and given this condition, returns the first page of matching rows. This doesn't need to use OFFSET at all because it's searching for the start of the set of rows by value, not by position.

Pagination/soln/keyset-fetch.sql

```
SELECT *
FROM comment
WHERE comment_id > 5
ORDER BY comment_id
FETCH FIRST 5 ROWS ONLY;
```

But comment_id values aren't necessarily consecutive. The value you use in the WHERE clause isn't always a multiple of the page size. What value could you use to start the range at the start of a given page?

When viewing the first page, this is easy—you want the query to start WHERE comment_id > 0.

Then, for the next page, use the value of comment_id on the last row fetched from the prior page. If your users typically start by viewing the first page, and then proceed to the immediate next page, you can pass the last comment_id value in the request for the next page. This way, each page request knows where to start.

The following figure shows that the rows examined for each page are the same as the rows returned by the query. No rows are examined unnecessarily.

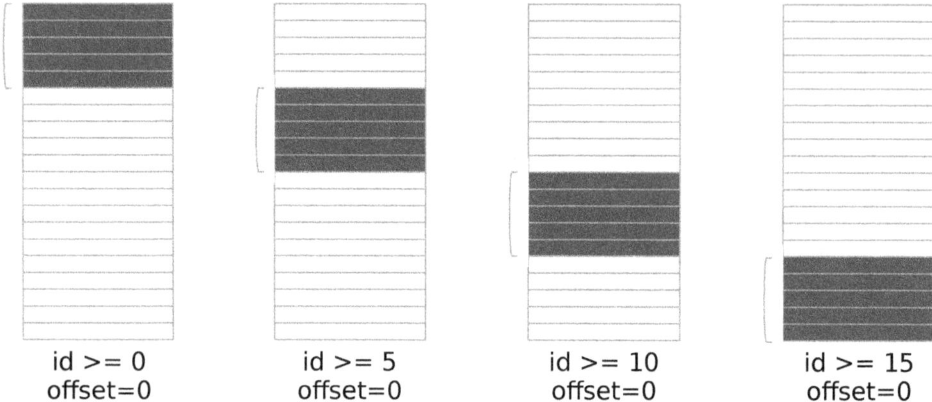

This solution is promising, as long as you keep some limitations in mind:

First, you can use this method only to request the next page following the page you are currently viewing. You can't skip pages because the current page only includes the last comment_id before the immediate next page starts. You can't navigate in reverse (in other words, to view the previous page) because the current page doesn't include the last comment_id from two pages prior.

Second, the column you use for the keyset pagination must be naturally ordered and contain no duplicates. Suppose the last comment_id value in the current page appears on several rows (perhaps because the query joined to another table with a one-to-many relationship), and these rows span over the boundary between the current page and the next page. The following figure shows a case where both the current page and the next page include rows with a comment_id value of 5.

current page

comment_id	reaction
4	Like
4	Like
5	LOL
5	Heart
5	LOL

last comment_id = 5

next page

comment_id	reaction
5	Heart
5	LOL
6	Like
6	Like
6	Like

WHERE comment_id > 5
skips some rows

If your query to get the next page uses WHERE comment_id > 5 because 5 is the last value of comment_id on the current page, then the next page will skip some rows it should have included. This problem won't happen if the column you use for the keyset pagination has no duplicates.

If your query has no column guaranteed to be unique, then the keyset pagination solution won't work.

Query Several Pages at Once

You may assume that in a typical application, a user never wants to view thousands of pages of results. It's more likely that a user views a small number of pages, and if they don't see what they want, they start over with a different search.

You can query to fetch several pages worth of data initially, and use that result as the user requests further pages. The fastest SQL query is the one you don't have to run at all because you've already saved the result from a prior SQL query. This is called a *cache*, a high-performance but ephemeral storage, that keeps a small data set available for the next few requests for subsequent pages. This will be covered in more detail in Chapter 10, Cacheless Transactions, on page 121.

The best number of pages for this initial query depends on your application and your user behavior. You can write code in your application to log how users request pages and gradually collect statistics about the maximum page most searches view. There will be a few outliers; a decreasing number of users view 10 or 20 or more pages. It's up to you to decide what you think is an appropriate number of pages, for example, enough to satisfy 95 percent of user searches without needing to fetch more data.

How do you do this in your application? Write one first query that reads the initial results, with a LIMIT of, say, 8–10 pages worth of rows. Fetch all the results, and store the rows in a cache.

The following Python Flask example shows that Visage code would prefer to read a dataset from the cache. If the dataset is not already in the cache, or if the user's request for the first page indicates they want a fresh view of the comments, then the code queries the database.

Pagination/soln/page-cache/app.py

```
from flask import Flask, request, render_template
from flask_caching import Cache
import psycopg2
import psycopg2.extras

app = Flask(__name__)
cache = Cache(app, config={'CACHE_TYPE': 'SimpleCache'})
```

```
@app.route("/comments", methods=['GET'])
def comments():
    page = request.args.get('page', default=1, type=int)

    comments_paged = cache.get('comments')

    if comments_paged is None or page == 1:
        comments_paged = get_comments()
        cache.set('comments', comments_paged)

    return render_template('comments.html',
                           comments=comments_paged[page],
                           next_page=page+1)

# fetch 10 pages of comments from database
# and separate into pages of 5 comments each
def get_comments():
    num_pages = 10
    page_size = 5

    comments_paged = [[]] * (num_pages+1)

    with psycopg2.connect("dbname='visage' host='localhost'") as conn:

        cur = conn.cursor(cursor_factory=psycopg2.extras.RealDictCursor)

        sql = f"""
            SELECT * FROM comment
            ORDER BY comment_id
            FETCH FIRST {num_pages * page_size} ROWS ONLY
        """
        cur.execute(sql)
        rows = cur.fetchall()

        for page in range(num_pages):
            start = page * page_size
            end = start + page_size
            comments_paged[page+1] = rows[start:end]

    return comments_paged

if __name__ == '__main__':
    app.run()
```

A simple HTML template for this view is as follows:

Pagination/soln/page-cache/templates/comments.html

```
<!DOCTYPE html>
<html>
<head><title>Visage Comments</title></head>
<body>
  <h1>Visage Comments</h1>

  <table border=1>
    <tr>
      <th>comment_id</th>
      <th>comment_text</th>
```

```
    </tr>
  {% for comment in comments %}
    <tr>
      <td>{{comment['comment_id']}}</td>
      <td>{{comment['comment_text']}}</td>
    </tr>
  {% endfor %}
  </table>

  <p><a href="?page={{next_page}}">Next Page</a></p>
</body>
</html>
```

The preceding code example is overly simplified because it is only to show a proof of concept of using a cache.

This solution works for some cases that keyset pagination does not. The user can skip pages or view previous pages. However, if the user requests pages beyond the set of cached pages, then the application must run another SQL query to fetch more data and add it to the cache. You may be able to prove through usage logs that it's rare for users to request more pages. The great majority of users experience a more optimized application.

Another Small Optimization

Some software developers advocate the following method to optimize the performance of pagination queries:

Pagination/soln/subquery.sql

```
SELECT * FROM (
  SELECT comment_id FROM comment
  ORDER BY comment_id
  OFFSET 10
  FETCH NEXT 5 ROWS ONLY
) AS c
JOIN comment USING (comment_id);
```

The idea is that because the subquery reads only the index, this may be less costly than paginating whole rows. Once the subquery returns a small set of primary key values for the desired page, these values are used to join to the respective rows, and thus, the query examines only rows that comprise the desired page.

It's true that the difference is measurable, but it's usually small. The subquery still has to work inefficiently to count entries from the start of the index. If the index is more compact than whole rows, this is a bit of savings. But at best, it improves latency by a fixed factor. The search is still linear and has the same complexity when expressed in big-O notation.[1]

Queries can be optimized to look up by value, but not by position.

Mini-Antipattern: LIMIT without ORDER BY

If you run any SELECT query, in what order does the SQL engine return the rows?

If you don't specify an order, the SQL engine is free to choose an arbitrary order. This varies by the implementation; in other words, PostgreSQL will be different from MySQL, and SQLite will be different still. It may also vary by other conditions in the query, or by other internal details of the SQL engine. You can't necessarily assume a query result will be in any reliable order, even with repeated executions of the same query.

This might not be important if you run a query that is not paginated. One way or another, you fetch the full result of a query, and you have an opportunity to reorder the result for display using application code if necessary.

But when running a pagination query, you request rows by their position, and you fetch a subset of them, so it's important to make their order consistent so the offset matches your desired position.

SQL queries have an optional ORDER BY clause. You should use this clause to define the order of rows explicitly, especially when writing pagination queries.

1. https://en.wikipedia.org/wiki/Big_O_notation

Part II

Optimization Antipatterns

As the saying goes, "make it work, make it right, then make it fast." An SQL query may work, but it doesn't necessarily come with optimal performance. It's important to be mindful of methods to optimize queries.

In mathematics, the art of asking questions is more valuable than solving problems.

Georg Cantor

CHAPTER 6

Non-Sargable Queries

Hayden, the intern software developer you've been mentoring, looks anxious. "I don't know how to solve this SQL query," he says.

"How can I help? Tell me what you're trying to do," you offer as you scoot your chair over to his desk.

Hayden takes in a deep breath and begins, "I have to develop a screen to display Visage posts for a given day. I was told the product manager needs this for a demo he's giving to a customer tomorrow morning. The post table has a timestamp column, which represents both date and time. So I tried to search by comparing the timestamp to a date value, like this:"

Non-Sargable/anti/created_at.sql

```
SELECT * FROM post
WHERE created_at = '2024-12-21';
```

"That won't return all rows for posts created on that date," you explain. "When comparing a timestamp to a date value, the SQL engine assumes you mean '2024-12-21 00:00:00' (midnight). Only posts with that exact timestamp would match. It's unlikely that any user created a post precisely at midnight that day."

"That's what I saw," Hayden continues. "So I thought of making the timestamp into a date, and comparing that to the value."

Non-Sargable/anti/date_cast.sql

```
SELECT * FROM post
WHERE CAST(created_at AS DATE) = '2024-12-21';
```

"This gives me the correct result—all posts created between midnight and the end of the following evening. But it's too slow to search that way."

"Even after you defined an index for the created_at column?" you ask.

"Yeah, it made no difference, and it's getting noticeably worse as the table gets larger." The intern's voice is shaky, and he glances at the clock.

You think for a moment and say, "Did you try using EXPLAIN to report the optimizer strategy for these two queries as I showed you yesterday?"

"Yes," he answers. "It uses the index in the first query, but that query doesn't return the rows I want. The second query doesn't use the index and falls back to a costly table scan. What can I do to solve this?"

Why doesn't the index help improve the performance of the second query? This chapter describes how to optimize these types of complex conditions in SQL queries.

Objective: Optimizing Complex Queries

After you learn to optimize straightforward SQL queries with conditions of the general form `WHERE column = value`, you still have to optimize SQL queries that are a little more complex and can't be written with simple conditions.

For example, in the anecdote for this chapter, the condition requires searching partial values stored in a column (extracting the date value from a timestamp). The same problem occurs when the search is for any other altered value, like an expression combining multiple columns, or another operation that modifies the value.

With a little thought, you can probably develop SQL code that works for the more "interesting" conditions, but making them optimized as well is not so easy.

Antipattern: Using Queries That Can't Be Optimized

SQL is an abstraction for data access. Before SQL was common, programmers had to read and write custom records in bespoke file formats. The purpose of SQL was to implement the reading and writing of records in a reusable way, allowing you to use the query syntax to describe the result you want using logical expressions. The SQL engine then takes care of finding the records you want, as efficiently as possible.

Most of the time, SQL succeeds at its mission. You don't have to think about the details of how the engine interprets the logic of a query, or how records are stored in a data file, in order to run a query that finds the records that match the conditions. But when it comes to optimization, the veneer of this abstraction weakens. To optimize complex searches, you need to know how the engine uses indexes.

A good analogy for this type of index is a telephone book, where the list of names has been sorted by last name, then by first name. If you search for a specific last name, you can find it efficiently because names in the index are alphabetized. The reason it's faster to search such an index is that you can depend on the fact that it was stored in sorted order.

If you search in a way that isn't guaranteed to match the sorted order of that index, then the index can't help to find matching names. For instance, a substring in the middle of a name would rarely have the same order as the full name.

These are called *non-sargable* queries.

What Does Sargable Mean?

The word "sargable" isn't a natural word; it's a neologism that appeared in the 1979 paper, *Access Path Selection in a Relational Database Management System [SACL79].*

The paper is about how an SQL engine would implement a search when conditions have the form `<column> <comparison-operator> <pattern>`.

For example, `created_at = '2024-12-21'` is this type of condition. The `<column>` is `created_at`, the `<comparison-operator>` is `=`, and the `<pattern>` is the constant value `'2024-12-21'`.

The condition is applied to each row in a table, and when the condition is true on a given row, that row is returned as part of the query result. The writers of the paper called this type of condition a *search argument*, or "SARG" for short.

According to the paper's authors, if that condition is of the SARG form, and the column on the left-hand side of the comparison operator matches the key of an index, then the optimizer can use that index. This likely gives the query improved performance because the index helps the search to find matching entries in logarithmic time instead of linear time. If a query uses such conditions, they called the query *sargable*.

Sargable has been used as a term for a query that may benefit from index optimization. But it's still an obscure word, even among database professionals.

A quick way to know if a query might be non-sargable is that a column in the search condition is used as an argument to a function, or is part of an expression on the left-hand side of the condition. The query you saw earlier is an example of using the column as a function argument.

Non-Sargable/anti/date_cast.sql

```
SELECT * FROM post
WHERE CAST(created_at AS DATE) = '2024-12-21';
```

The following query is an example of using an expression on the left-hand side of the condition. It searches for posts written more than a week ago. The expression adds one week to the created_at timestamp. If that's greater than or equal to the current timestamp, then the post is at least seven days old.

Non-Sargable/anti/date_add.sql
```
SELECT * FROM post
WHERE created_at + INTERVAL '7' DAY >= CURRENT_TIMESTAMP;
```

There are exceptions to this guideline for identifying a non-sargable query, as you'll see in the solution section of this chapter.

How to Recognize the Antipattern

- "I created an index on the created_at column, but the query won't use the index!"

  You need to confirm that the expression in that query is logically able to use an index.

- "How can I search efficiently for telephone prefix numbers?"

  Many such cases can be solved in another way. For example, a telephone number could be separated into its components and stored as separate columns.

Legitimate Uses of the Antipattern

Non-sargable query conditions work in that they produce the result matching the logic of the query. They just don't use an index for that condition. This might be acceptable if the query examines a relatively small table.

Your query might also have other conditions that do use an index, narrowing down the search enough that applying the non-sargable condition to a small set of examined rows is perfectly fine.

Suppose the following query searches for a specific user who wrote posts (assume an index exists for user_id, to optimize that condition). Then the query filters the result by posts that were written on a specific date. The second condition works, but it's non-sargable.

Non-Sargable/soln/two_conditions.sql
```
SELECT * FROM post
WHERE user_id = 1234
  AND CAST(created_at AS DATE) = '2024-12-21';
```

If the search by user matches a small enough subset of the rows in your table, that may be enough to ensure the query has acceptable performance. You don't necessarily gain much better performance by optimizing the second condition.

Solution: Refactoring the Query

If your query's conditions are already in a sargable form (<column> <comparison-operator> <pattern>), then it's easy to create an index where the <column> of the condition is the leftmost column of the index.

In cases where a query has conditions that are not sargable, you need another solution.

The first thing to keep in mind is that although SQL is supposed to be an abstraction layer, the reality is that every implementation of an abstraction is imperfect. This means that optimizing a query sometimes means you have to write the syntax differently. In theory, two queries that return the same result should be run by the SQL engine with the same efficiency, and the abstraction should free you from needing to know how it does this. But in practice, one query may be easier for the SQL implementation to optimize. Some implementations are more clever at optimizing certain types of queries, but no implementation can optimize every type of query.

You can change most non-sargable queries into sargable queries. The following sections show solutions for doing that.

Rewriting Expressions

Many non-sargable queries can be rewritten into a form that is sargable. For example, recall the query for posts on a given date:

```
SELECT * FROM post
WHERE CAST(created_at AS DATE) = '2024-12-21';
```

This can be rewritten in the following way, which is sargable because the indexed column is alone on the left side of the comparison operator, but it also matches the range of timestamps for the whole day.

Non-Sargable/soln/date_between.sql

```
SELECT * FROM post
WHERE created_at BETWEEN '2024-12-21 00:00:00' AND '2024-12-22 23:59:59';
```

If timestamps support fractional seconds, the preceding query excludes almost the full second right before midnight, from '23:59:59.001' to '23:59:59.999'. There's a better habit: instead of using BETWEEN, search for timestamps strictly less than '00:00:00' of the following day, as in the following example:

Non-Sargable/soln/date_range.sql

```
SELECT * FROM post
WHERE created_at >= '2024-12-21 00:00:00'
  AND created_at < '2024-12-22 00:00:00';
```

For columns in an expression on the left-hand side of the comparison, in many cases, you can use algebra to isolate the column on the left-hand side, and a constant expression on the right-hand side, as in the following query:

Non-Sargable/soln/date_add_sargable.sql
```
SELECT * FROM post
WHERE created_at >= CURRENT_TIMESTAMP - INTERVAL '7' DAY;
```

Not all queries can be rewritten to be sargable. For example, suppose your task is to search for posts that were written in the month of December of any year. The non-sargable query would be the following:

Non-Sargable/soln/created_at_december.sql
```
SELECT * FROM post
WHERE EXTRACT(MONTH FROM created_at) = 12;
```

You can't rewrite this using BETWEEN, as in the example of searching for a specific day. An index on a date or timestamp is ordered by year first, then by month. This means the entries for December in the current year are not contiguous with the entries for December in any other year, so the index is not used.

Another case is if the condition compares multiple columns, then an index on the first column cannot optimize the query. For example, the following query matches posts that have been updated since they were created:

Non-Sargable/soln/updated_at.sql
```
SELECT * FROM post
WHERE created_at < updated_at;
```

That query isn't searching for a fixed value in the created_at column. It needs to search for a potentially different value on each row, so it needs to compare created_at to updated_at row by row.

Using Expression Indexes

An alternative to refactoring the query syntax is to create an index for the result of an expression. Even if the table doesn't store the same values, the index stores them.

You can create an expression index that calls a function, as in the following example:

Non-Sargable/soln/date_cast_index.sql
```
CREATE INDEX post_created_date ON post ((CAST(created_at AS DATE)));

-- uses the index
SELECT * FROM post
WHERE CAST(created_at AS DATE) = '2024-12-21';
```

After creating the expression index, a query can use that index if it searches with the same expression as the index definition—even if the expression is on the left-hand side of the comparison operator. This is an exception to the rule that the left-hand operand must be a bare column reference.

This solution works for other expressions, but not all queries can be optimized with an expression index. The following example is contrived, but it demonstrates a case that doesn't work:

Non-Sargable/soln/date_add_index.sql

```
CREATE INDEX post_created_1week ON post ((created_at + INTERVAL '7' DAY));

-- uses the index
SELECT * FROM post
WHERE created_at + INTERVAL '7' DAY >= CURRENT_TIMESTAMP;

-- does not use the index
SELECT * FROM post
WHERE created_at + INTERVAL '14' DAY >= CURRENT_TIMESTAMP;
```

The '7' DAY offset is fixed in the index definition, and this index only helps optimize queries that use the exact same expression. If you need to query for a different offset, it doesn't match, so the index can't be used. In general, any arguments besides the referenced column must be exactly the same value as used in the index definition.

Expression indexes do help optimize some queries that can't be optimized by rewriting the query. For example, the query that compared created_at to updated_at can be indexed as follows:

Non-Sargable/soln/updated_at_index.sql

```
CREATE INDEX post_updated ON post ((created_at < updated_at));

-- uses the index in PostgreSQL, but not in MySQL
SELECT * FROM post
WHERE created_at < updated_at;

-- uses the index in both PostgreSQL and MySQL
SELECT * FROM post
WHERE (created_at < updated_at) = true;
```

Note the difference when using MySQL's implementation: the query has to be written slightly differently than the original non-sargable query. Using a Boolean expression like created_at < updated_at doesn't work because it isn't in the form of <column> <comparison-operator> <pattern>. With expression indexes, the <column> part of that form can be replaced by the expression used for the index, but depending on the specific product, the other parts of the form still need to be there.

Which Databases Support Expression Indexes?

The feature of expression indexes is not defined in the ANSI/ISO SQL standard. In fact, if you read the section "Indexes Aren't Standard" in *SQL Antipatterns Volume 1 [Kar22]*, then you may recall that the SQL standard does not describe indexes of any kind. All syntax and implementation for indexes is a vendor-specific extension to standard SQL, and each vendor has developed features they think are of most value to their customers.

So, it's not surprising that support for expression indexes is not consistent between brands. Many brands support expression indexes more or less as described in this chapter, as of the following releases:

- PostgreSQL 7.0 (2000)
- Oracle 8i (2000)
- Informix 9.40 (2003)
- IBM DB2 10.5 (2013)
- SQLite 3.9.0 (2015)
- MySQL 8.0 (2018)

Some brands support expression indexes indirectly. You first define a *generated column* in a table, then you can create an index for the values in the generated column. Brands that use this implementation include:

- Microsoft SQL Server 8 (2000) through at least 17 (2025)
- MySQL 5.7 (2015)

Storing Customized Data

A further solution you can use is to define a new column and store modified values derived from one or more existing columns in a way that supports indexed searches.

In some cases, you can use a generated column:

Non-Sargable/soln/date_cast_gen.sql

```
ALTER TABLE post ADD COLUMN created_at_date DATE
  GENERATED ALWAYS AS (CAST(created_at AS DATE)) STORED;

CREATE INDEX post_created ON post (created_at_date);

SELECT * FROM post
WHERE created_at_date = '2024-12-21';
```

Generated columns keep their value in sync every time the row is updated. They have some limitations, such as they can't use nondeterministic functions, subqueries, or reference data in any row other than the row they are calculating.

You have the option to take responsibility for keeping such a column updated, using triggers or your own code. This opens up opportunities for storing data that are derived in ways that generated columns can't be. This is an example of denormalization, which is covered in more detail in Chapter 7, Premature Denormalization, on page 67.

SQL is an abstraction for query results, but when it comes to optimization, be mindful of implementation details.

Mini-Antipattern: Redundant Indexes

Some SQL engines allow you to create more than one index on the same columns, or on a superset of columns. These indexes are redundant. There's no benefit to keeping both of them.

There are a few disadvantages of redundant indexes, which might be important to your application:

- Indexes consume storage space, just like the table itself.
- Indexes need to be updated when you INSERT, UPDATE, or DELETE a row.
- Indexes must be considered by the query optimizer, so the more indexes, the more complex the optimizer's job is.

The simplest case is when two indexes have exactly the same columns. One of the indexes is redundant and you can drop it. Then you can consider cases where indexes don't have exactly the same columns, but one is a subset of the other.

Suppose the post table has these two nonunique indexes:

```
CREATE INDEX post_usr_cr ON post (user_id, created_at);
CREATE INDEX post_usr_cr_up ON post (user_id, created_at, updated_at);
```

A query that needs to query the first two columns can use the index with three columns and simply ignore the third column of the index. So, you can drop the post_usr_cr index, as long as its columns are the left-most subset of columns of the post_usr_cr_up index.

Unique indexes are different. Suppose the post table must restrict a user to post only once per timestamp. This is enforced with a unique index:

```
CREATE UNIQUE INDEX post_usr_cr_uniq ON post (user_id, created_at);
CREATE UNIQUE INDEX post_usr_cr_up_uniq ON post (user_id, created_at,
  updated_at);
```

The unique index with three columns is redundant because if there is a unique index on two of those columns, then there's already a constraint that only one row can exist for given values in those two columns. Therefore, it's never possible for more than one row to exist with given values in the three columns of the second unique index. The three-column unique index is redundant and can be dropped. If any subset of the columns comprises a unique constraint, then the unique index with more columns can be dropped. The subset doesn't have to be left-most, or in any order.

ANSI/ISO SQL-compliant databases have views to metadata called INFORMATION_SCHEMA, but as mentioned earlier in the chapter, indexes are not features of ANSI/ISO SQL. The metadata about indexes and their columns isn't in the standard views. Each brand of SQL database may extend these views with its own design. In the case of PostgreSQL, metadata about indexes, columns, and tables are in the pg_catalog schema.

Were it not sinful then, striving to mend,
To mar the subject that before was well?

William Shakespeare, Sonnet 103

CHAPTER 7

Premature Denormalization

Siobhán's face appears over your monitor. She's the manager of the group that engineers reports and monitoring. "Got a moment? We apparently have a problem in the database," she says. Next to her is J.P., the director of finance. You suddenly sense that your answer to Siobhán's question had better be yes.

"How can I help?" you ask, showing that you are giving her your full attention.

Siobhán begins, "I recall you stored the quarterly total revenue in the database."

"Right, that was to optimize the sales dashboard," you explain. "As sales are booked, the total is recalculated, and the dashboard reads the total. It was too slow when we queried the whole table every time the dashboard refreshed. Is the dashboard too slow again?"

"No, the dashboard is quick enough," she continues. "But the total doesn't match the sales data." J.P. is looking at you with a stern expression on their face.

You gradually remember that the dashboard code was recently refactored by an engineer who left the company suddenly last week. He changed a lot of code, and his changes slipped through the normal code review process. Since it was only the dashboard, no one felt it was worth fighting over enforcing that process.

"Okay, we can add a backlog item to revisit the dashboard code," you suggest, trying to avoid blame.

"You don't understand," J.P. says. "My team used the number on the dashboard for our revenue reporting, which has already gone out. Now that we discovered that it's way off from the true total, we have to refile that report. The finance team will have to work through the weekend, but that's not the worst part. The company is being scrutinized by stock market analysts, and this unexpected change makes it look like we're deliberately reporting inaccurate numbers."

Siobhán explains, "It doesn't matter whether the change goes up or down; it will probably affect our stock price."

The finance director nods, and they add, "And it may trigger a full audit."

Objective: Breaking the Rules to Improve Performance

As always, it's about performance. Developers seek any method they can use to optimize their database, even if it means breaking the rules in creative ways.

In a relational database, the rules of normalization help us to design tables and columns in a way that minimizes redundancy and reduces the chance of data anomalies. Read more about normalization in the appendix "Rules of Normalization" in *SQL Antipatterns Volume 1 [Kar22]*.

Rules can be broken, and if doing so means even a slight improvement to performance, it's easy to justify. This is where *denormalization* can provide value, if used wisely.

If not used wisely, any method of optimization—including denormalization—can cause new problems. That's what this chapter is about.

Antipattern: Breaking the Rules Recklessly

"Normalize until it hurts, denormalize until it works," has been written many times, for example, in Jeff Atwood's 2008 blog "Maybe Normalizing Isn't Normal."[1] A well-chosen exception to the rules might give big rewards. The problem is that when a trick works well once, you're tempted to use it more and more. In the case of denormalization, some software developers start to prefer it over the standard practice, and they use it too liberally.

Let's look at examples of forms of denormalization to show the problems you can cause.

Avoiding Joins, Part 1

Chapter 2, Fear of JOINs, on page 11 showed that joins can be optimized, and it's a good way to return attributes of related tables. But reading two or more rows from different tables is more costly than reading one row from a single table (this depends on the SQL implementation, but it's true in most

1. https://blog.codinghorror.com/maybe-normalizing-isnt-normal/

OLTP database products). If you've tried to improve a join query with indexes and it's still too inefficient, you might be tempted to store an attribute in the table you mean to join to, instead of the table where rules of normalization would guide you to put that attribute.

For example, suppose you need to write an SQL query to show a post with its author's name. The user name is normally stored in the user table, but that makes you join the tables.

Denormalization/anti/normal-join.sql
```
SELECT p.post_title, u.display_name
FROM post AS p JOIN "user" AS u USING (user_id)
WHERE p.post_id = 1234;
```

So, you try to move the user name into the post table. You can visualize what you want to do: the name that exists for a given user_id in the user table, copy it to a new column in the respective row of the post table that references that user.

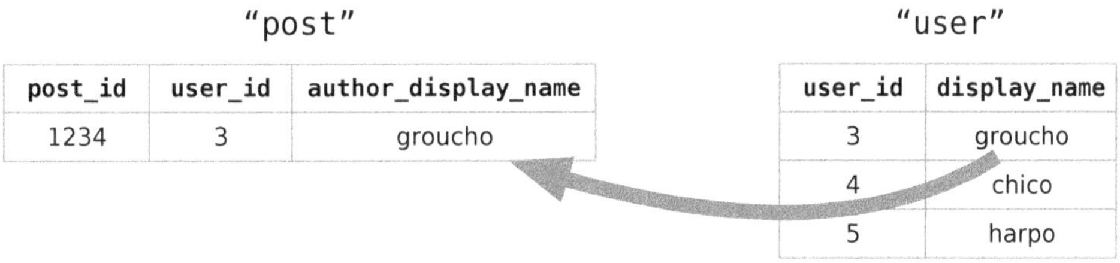

"post"

post_id	user_id	author_display_name
1234	3	groucho

"user"

user_id	display_name
3	groucho
4	chico
5	harpo

In SQL, that operation looks like the following:

Denormalization/anti/avoid-join.sql
```
ALTER TABLE post ADD COLUMN author_display_name VARCHAR(64);

UPDATE post SET author_display_name = 'Groucho'
WHERE post_id = 1234;
```

Now, you can query the author name from the post table, without doing a join:

Denormalization/anti/avoid-join.sql
```
SELECT p.post_title, p.author_display_name
FROM post AS p
WHERE post_id = 1234;
```

But if the user wants to change their display name, it becomes more work to update it. You'd have to update the user table, as you normally would, and potentially many rows in the post table.

You could create a trigger to update copies of the display name in the other table when the user changes it. Then you might wonder if there are other tables in this database that have their own copy of the user display name.

Your trigger would have to be coded to update all those other tables. Everything is possible, but the point is that the more you denormalize, the more extra work you have to do to maintain those copies.

An alternative would be to skip changing the display name for old posts. Only new posts written after the name change would get the new name. That would make the same user appear using different display names in different posts, which would be confusing for users of Visage.

Avoiding Joins, Part 2

A post in Visage can be assigned one or more tags to help readers search for posts they're interested in. So, you have a requirement to display the tags for a given post. Posts and tags have a many-to-many relationship. That is, a post may have multiple tags, and a given tag may apply to multiple posts. In a normalized database, you'd create a third table and save each pairing as a row. Now, you have to make *two* joins to show a post with its tags:

Denormalization/anti/normal-join-many.sql

```
SELECT p.post_title, t.tag
FROM post AS p LEFT JOIN post_tag AS pt USING (post_id)
LEFT JOIN tag AS t USING (tag_id)
WHERE p.post_id = 1234;
```

If you could denormalize by storing the list of tags in the post table, you'd skip those joins and get the list directly when you display the post. Suppose you copied a set of tag IDs from multiple rows into a single row, as illustrated by the following diagram:

In SQL, you write it like the following:

Denormalization/anti/avoid-join-many.sql

```
-- Add the column once
ALTER TABLE post ADD COLUMN tag_list VARCHAR(64);

-- Set the list each time you add or remove a tag
UPDATE post SET tag_list = 'tag1,tag2,tag5'
WHERE post_id = 1234;
```

```
-- Then subsequently get the list any time you query
SELECT p.post_title, p.tag_list
FROM post AS p
WHERE post_id = 1234;
```

This leads to new problems. The first is that the items in the comma-separated string don't necessarily match the values in the original post_tag table. If you were to add a new tag or remove a tag for a given post, you'd have to update both tables, and if you forget, then the lists will be out of sync. The problem is, you can't tell which is correct—the comma-separated string, or the rows in the post_tag table. Which one failed to be updated? Was a new tag added to post.tag_list, or was a row deleted from post_tag?

You could solve this by eliminating the post_tag table. Storing the tags for a post in two places risks them getting out of sync, so make sure the tags for a given post are stored in one place. This causes a new problem: if you need to search for posts by tag instead of by primary key, you can't easily optimize searching for substrings in a comma-separated list. PostgreSQL has support for arrays, and an operator && that tests if two arrays overlap. The following example shows how you could write the query in PostgreSQL:

Denormalization/anti/avoid-join-many-by-tag.sql
```
SELECT p.post_title, p.tag_list
FROM post AS p
WHERE regexp_split_to_array(p.tag_list, ',') && '{"tag5"}';
```

Standard SQL supports the ARRAY data type and a function ANY(). The following example shows how you could write such a query:

Denormalization/anti/avoid-join-many-by-array.sql
```
-- Add the column once
ALTER TABLE post ADD COLUMN tag_array VARCHAR(64)[1000];

-- Set the list each time you add or remove a tag
UPDATE post SET tag_array = ARRAY['tag1','tag2','tag5']
WHERE post_id = 1234;

SELECT p.post_title, p.tag_array
FROM post AS p
WHERE 'tag5' = ANY(p.tag_array);
```

However, PostgreSQL can't use an index in either of the preceding queries. If you still had the normalized table, you could write a query that's easier to optimize:

Denormalization/anti/normal-join-many-by-tag.sql
```
SELECT p.post_title, t.tag
FROM post AS p JOIN post_tag AS pt USING (post_id)
JOIN tag AS t USING (tag_id)
WHERE t.tag_id = 5;
```

In addition, there are many problems with storing values as comma-separated lists. The length of the VARCHAR creates an unnecessary limit to the number of tags. The items in the string aren't constrained to be valid tags. The string itself isn't even constrained to be formatted as a comma-separated list. See the chapter "Jaywalking" in *SQL Antipatterns Volume 1 [Kar22]* for the full story.

Avoiding Aggregation

Visage posts can be rated by other users. A user rates a post with a numeric value between 0 and 5 (5 is the most favorable), and each user's rating is stored as a row in the rating table. When you display a post, you'd like to show the average of all ratings given by users for that post. The SQL query uses AVG(rating) to calculate a single aggregate value from the group:

Denormalization/anti/normal-agg.sql

```
SELECT p.post_id, AVG(r.rating) AS avg_rating
FROM post AS p JOIN rating AS r USING (post_id)
WHERE p.post_id = 1234
GROUP BY p.post_id;
```

Suppose this query is too slow, since some posts could be rated by many users. The aggregation needs to examine many rows from the rating table, and that might be too slow. So, you decide to calculate the average once and store it as an attribute column in the post table.

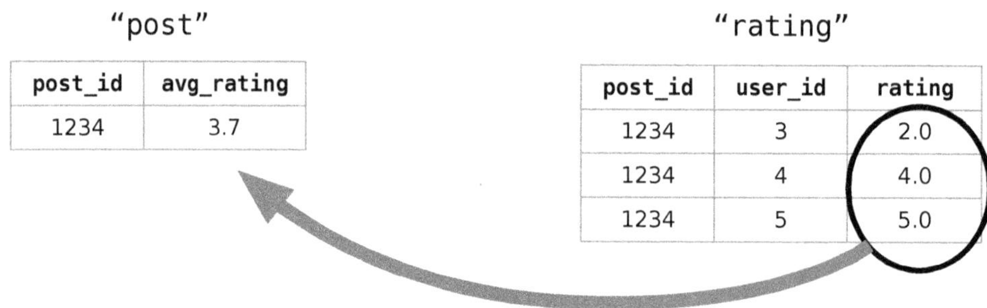

Denormalization/anti/avoid-agg.sql

```
ALTER TABLE post ADD COLUMN avg_rating NUMERIC(2,1);
```

Now, you can query just one row when you need to show that average rating:

Denormalization/anti/avoid-agg.sql

```
SELECT post_id, avg_rating
FROM post
WHERE post_id = 1234;
```

This is a problem because if another user subsequently gives a rating for that post, it would likely make the stored average inaccurate (unless their rating was by coincidence equal to the stored average). To ensure the stored average was accurate, you'd have to recalculate it after every user inserts or updates their rating.

In this example of recalculating an average, you could get a new average if you also store the number of existing ratings, as well as the average. From these two values, you would multiply the current average by the number of ratings, then add the new rating to make a new sum, and divide by the incremented number of ratings. If you could do that, then why have a separate `rating` table at all? You might choose to drop the `rating` table and keep only the denormalized average and rating count in the `post` table.

In practice, bugs can and do happen. Suppose you notice a miscalculation (for example, if the average were 3.6, this can't be the result of an average of three whole numbers between 1 and 5). Either the average is incorrect, or the number of ratings is incorrect, but you don't know which. If you had dropped the `rating` table and lost all the individual ratings, you can't resolve this error.

You might also need to record each user's rating separately to allow users to change their rating.

Similar problems happen if you store the result of any other type of aggregate calculation, for example, a `SUM()` of a group of payments in a ledger or a `COUNT()` of posts made in a day.

Avoiding Calculations

Displaying a post in Visage also needs to show the age of the post, for example, "6 days ago." This is an opportunity to use a third type of denormalization for expressions calculated in the select-list of a query. This is admittedly a less common type of denormalization, but it's possible that the expression is complex enough to be costly and slow.

For this example, the expression is relatively simple:

Denormalization/anti/avoid-expr.sql

```
SELECT post_id, EXTRACT(DAY FROM CURRENT_TIMESTAMP - created_at) AS age
FROM post
WHERE post_id = 1234;
```

But suppose you had to eliminate that expression from the query; you might store the age as a column:

Denormalization/anti/avoid-expr.sql
```
ALTER TABLE post ADD COLUMN age NUMERIC;

UPDATE post SET age = EXTRACT(DAY FROM CURRENT_TIMESTAMP - created_at)
```

Then, the query would read the pre-calculated value from the column, instead of calculating it during the query:

Denormalization/anti/avoid-expr.sql
```
SELECT post_id, age
FROM post
WHERE post_id = 1234;
```

You can probably easily see the pitfall in this example: the age attribute is accurate only on the day you added that column and calculated the age. If you query the age tomorrow, it will still have the value you set it to today, and that won't reflect the true age, which should be one day more.

This example is meant to show clearly that storing the result of an expression can become inaccurate.

As mentioned in Chapter 6, Non-Sargable Queries, on page 57, some SQL products support generated columns. You could add a column that is bound to be recalculated if any other columns change. But generated columns can only reference other columns in the same row, or certain built-in SQL functions. They can't reference other rows, other tables, or nondeterministic SQL functions.

Triggers may also recalculate expressions during an INSERT or UPDATE, and this allows more types of expressions that read multiple rows, or other tables, or any SQL function or user-defined function. But this still wouldn't help make the age column stay accurate. Nor would a trigger help if part of the expression depends on other rows (for example, recalculating the price of an order based on taxes, which change).

The Bottom Line

While denormalization appears to give a benefit at first, you can see now that there's a trade-off with regard to data integrity.

Denormalization helps to optimize one type of query, but at the same time penalizes other queries or requires additional queries to search for inaccuracies and correct them.

You can also encounter cases where it's hard to know which copy of the data is correct and which needs to be fixed. Sometimes, this can't be automated; it requires a person to exercise their judgment.

How to Recognize the Antipattern

- "Denormalization makes databases faster, so do it as much as possible."

  A specific use of denormalization may help a specific query, but this isn't a general solution to optimize all queries.

- "Why doesn't this calculated field add up to the same sum as the original data?"

  Redundant copies of the same data are susceptible to getting out of sync as they change.

- "How can we track who changed the data? We need to know so we can decide which copy is more recent."

  When data get out of sync, it's a challenge to know which copy is correct.

Legitimate Uses of the Antipattern

It's worthwhile to structure data in a way that improves the efficiency of the work you need to do with those data.

Rob Pike wrote in his essay, "Notes on Programming in C":[2]

> Data dominates. If you've chosen the right data structures and organized things well, the algorithms will almost always be self-evident. Data structures, not algorithms, are central to programming.

Denormalization is a practical application of Pike's philosophy. If you transform data into a structure that assists a specific query, then that query (the algorithm in Pike's statement) may run more efficiently. But a different query may need a different structure.

Dimensional modeling is a form of denormalization, where tables are designed to support a specific reporting query. Ralph Kimball has written many books, for example, *The Data Warehouse Toolkit: The Definitive Guide to Dimensional Modeling, Third Edition [Kim13]*. Kimball's process for building a dimensional model starts with identifying the business process, which is more or less another way of saying start with the query.

If you need a variety of different reports—for instance, in Visage, you might need a report on user activity, and another report to measure popularity by post—then you may need multiple dimensional models. Each one stores the same data, but in a different denormalized way.

---

2. https://doc.cat-v.org/bell_labs/pikestyle

Solution: Breaking the Rules Carefully

Even if you succeed in using denormalization to optimize queries, this always complicates your database and increases the cost and the risk of mistakes and anomalies described in the antipattern section of this chapter. Any kind of risk in your project needs to be managed and justified.

You can make denormalization less painful and costly using two methods: choosing the right time to use this method, and mitigating the risks with defensive programming. Let's explore those two methods.

Choosing the Right Time to Denormalize

There are several questions you should ask before deciding to change your tables to a denormalized form.

Do you have a specific SQL query to optimize?

Having a specific query is important because you can't choose how to make the denormalized version of the table without a concrete case to optimize. In the antipattern section, we saw cases of specific queries that produced the correct result, even though they may have had performance issues, or writing the query was too complex. That's the right place to start from because, as you design a query for the denormalized table, you can compare the result of the new query to the original one.

Attempting to denormalize without a specific query in mind would be like trying to fix a bug that has no description or reproducible test case.

Have you tried other methods of optimizing that query?

Having tried other optimizations first is important because if you can achieve the performance goal while using normal tables, you can avoid the maintenance of the denormalized tables. Other methods include adding indexes, refactoring the query syntax, omitting columns you don't need in the result, changing data types, or partitioning the table.

Can you confirm that denormalization does, in fact, meet your performance goal?

Measure the performance of the query you need to optimize. The simplest way to do this is by writing code in your application to get the clock time before you execute the query, and saving that value in a variable. Then, get the clock time again after the query is done, and compare the two times:

Denormalization/soln/timing.py

```
import psycopg2
import time

conn = psycopg2.connect("dbname='visage' host='localhost'")

with conn.cursor() as cur:

    t0 = time.perf_counter()

    cur.execute("""
        UPDATE "user"
        SET display_name = 'julius'
        WHERE user_id = 3;
    """)

    t1 = time.perf_counter()

    elapsed = t1 - t0
    print(f'Elapsed time of query: {elapsed:.6f} seconds')

# Output:
# Elapsed time of query: 0.019050 seconds
```

Then, implement a prototype of the denormalized table, and try a refactored SQL query against it. Again, measure the time duration of the query. How much has it improved? Does this meet your performance goal?

If the denormalized table still can't reach your goal, then you shouldn't add the complexity of maintaining it to your project. Take a step back and consider other options. Do you really need to run this query? Can you rethink your application so it doesn't need the data, or can it use data previously saved in the cache?

There are more sophisticated tools to profile code execution time in an application, but these depend on the language and development environment you use. Read other resources to learn about the best performance measurement tools. For example, if you use Ruby, read *Ruby Performance Optimization [Dym15]*.

Are you ready to commit to maintaining the denormalized table?

It's important that you make an intentional and realistic plan to keep the denormalization operational. As you saw in the antipattern section, data can get out of sync easily, and it's not always clear how to fix it when that happens. Someone needs to do ongoing work to preserve data integrity because the database software can't do that.

Mitigating Risks with Defensive Programming

Once you've decided to use denormalization, the following habits help you to be smart about implementing it, to reduce the chances of mistakes and manage their impact.

Automating Synchronous Updates

Your goal is to keep the denormalized data in sync as you change the normalized data.

One way to do this is by using a trigger. Suppose that in the Visage user table, when a user changes their name, you want the copy of their name in all of their posts to be updated at the same time. You could write the following trigger in PostgreSQL to do this:

Denormalization/soln/trigger-join.sql

```
CREATE OR REPLACE FUNCTION upd_denorm_user_name()
  RETURNS TRIGGER AS $$
BEGIN
  UPDATE post
  SET author_display_name = NEW.display_name
  WHERE user_id = NEW.user_id;

  RETURN NEW;
END;
$$ LANGUAGE PLPGSQL;

CREATE TRIGGER trig_denorm_user_name
  AFTER UPDATE ON "user"
FOR EACH ROW
  EXECUTE FUNCTION upd_denorm_user_name();
```

Test this trigger by first looking at the user display name in the denormalized post table:

Denormalization/soln/trigger-join.sql

```
SELECT post_id, user_id, author_display_name FROM post
WHERE user_id = 3;
```

post_id	user_id	author_display_name
1234	3	groucho

Then update the name in the user table. After the trigger does its work, the updated name has been copied to the post table:

Denormalization/soln/trigger-join.sql

```
UPDATE "user"
SET display_name = 'julius'
WHERE user_id = 3;
```

```
SELECT post_id, user_id, author_display_name FROM post
WHERE user_id = 3;
```

post_id	user_id	author_display_name
1234	3	julius

Let's look at another example of a trigger, this time for calculating the average rating for posts:

Denormalization/soln/trigger-agg.sql

```
CREATE OR REPLACE FUNCTION func_avg_rating()
  RETURNS TRIGGER AS $$
DECLARE
  new_post_id BIGINT := 0;
  old_post_id BIGINT := 0;
BEGIN

  IF (TG_OP IN ('INSERT', 'UPDATE')) THEN
    new_post_id := NEW.post_id;
  END IF;
  IF (TG_OP IN ('UPDATE', 'DELETE')) THEN
    old_post_id := OLD.post_id;
  END IF;

  WITH r(post_id, avg_rating) AS (
    SELECT post_id, AVG(rating)
    FROM rating
    WHERE post_id IN (new_post_id, old_post_id)
    GROUP BY post_id)
  UPDATE post
  SET avg_rating = r.avg_rating
  FROM r
  WHERE post.post_id = r.post_id;

  RETURN NEW;
END;
$$ LANGUAGE PLPGSQL;

CREATE TRIGGER trig_avg_rating
  AFTER INSERT OR UPDATE OR DELETE ON rating
FOR EACH ROW
  EXECUTE FUNCTION func_avg_rating();
```

First, check the initial data, and see the current average value:

Denormalization/soln/trigger-agg.sql

```
SELECT post_id, avg_rating FROM post
WHERE post_id = 1234;
```

post_id	avg_rating
1234	3.0

When you insert into or delete from the rating table, the trigger recalculates the average stored in the respective row of the post table:

Denormalization/soln/trigger-agg.sql
```
INSERT INTO rating (post_id, user_id, rating) VALUES (1234, 5, 5.0);

SELECT post_id, avg_rating FROM post
WHERE post_id = 1234;
```

post_id	avg_rating
1234	3.7

Denormalization/soln/trigger-agg.sql
```
DELETE FROM rating
WHERE post_id = 1234 AND user_id = 3;

SELECT post_id, avg_rating FROM post
WHERE post_id = 1234;
```

post_id	avg_rating
1234	4.5

An alternative, if you don't like writing triggers, is to execute two updates yourself from application code. Execute one update against the normal table and a second update against the copy in the denormalized table. You can do the two updates in a transaction to ensure both are committed together. In Python's db.SQL interface, a context manager (the with conn block) implicitly begins a transaction and commits it if no errors occur:

Denormalization/soln/two-updates.py
```
import psycopg2

conn = psycopg2.connect("dbname='visage' host='localhost'")

with conn:

    with conn.cursor() as cur:

        cur.execute("""
            UPDATE "user"
            SET display_name = 'julius'
            WHERE user_id = 3;
        """)

        cur.execute("""
            UPDATE post
            SET author_display_name = 'julius'
            WHERE user_id = 3;
        """)
```

Both the trigger solution and the two-updates solution have the advantage that the changes are made in the same transaction; no other session can see one change without the other. However, a disadvantage of doing two writes is that it adds a little overhead to your transaction. You must compare any benefit you get from the denormalized table to the extra cost of doing the update.

Triggers have an advantage over making two updates in application code. If you make such updates in multiple places in your application, or if you have multiple applications updating the same table, you'd have to repeat the same code in several places. You'd have a risk of forgetting to change one of the places where the update happens, which means occasionally the denormalized column in the post table won't be updated as you intended, whereas a trigger runs if any application updates the user table—or even if a developer runs a custom update from a script or an interactive client interface. This can help avoid some maddening bugs.

Automating Asynchronous Updates

Suppose you want the benefit of the denormalized post table, but you don't want the overhead of doing double writes during updates. There is a solution for this: asynchronous scheduled updates.

The following Python script updates any rows in post that aren't in sync with the current display name in user:

Denormalization/soln/update-display-name.py

```
import psycopg2

conn = psycopg2.connect("dbname='visage' host='localhost'")

with conn:

    with conn.cursor() as cur:

        cur.execute("""
            UPDATE post
            SET author_display_name = display_name
            FROM "user"
            WHERE post.user_id = "user".user_id;
        """)
```

On Linux, MacOS, and UNIX, a simple and standard way to execute a command on a schedule is with the cron command. You write a text file with a line that describes the schedule and the command to run. The following example runs every five minutes, every hour, every day, every week, every month.

Denormalization/soln/update-display-name.crontab

```
*/5 * * * * /usr/local/bin/update-display-name.py
```

Advantages of using the scheduled job include that your transaction that updates the user table doesn't bear the extra cost of updating the post table. Also, it works regardless of how the user table was updated; any client can make a change, and the asynchronous task should copy it.

However, there's a delay of up to five minutes after you update the user table before that change is copied to the post table. That may or may not be acceptable for a given project or even individual cases of denormalization within a project.

Also, if the script fails (for example, if the database is relocated or renamed, but you forget to update the script with the new connection arguments), then the post table would remain unchanged and out of sync with the recent change in the user table.

Implementing Quality Control

If you're worried about copies of data getting out of sync with the canonical data they're based on, you can implement code to check for that. For each case of denormalization in your tables, write a query to compare the copy with the original. If they aren't what you expect, then the code reports the discrepancies, and you must decide what to do.

The following code is an example of a check that you could implement if you denormalized the Visage user display name, as you saw earlier in this chapter. The user display names are supposed to be the same in both tables if the data are in sync. If they differ, then they should be reported. This query uses the NULL-safe comparison predicate IS DISTINCT FROM because either name could be NULL:

Denormalization/soln/check-avoid-join.sql

```
SELECT p.post_id, p.user_id, p.author_display_name, u.display_name
FROM post AS p JOIN "user" AS u USING (user_id)
WHERE p.author_display_name IS DISTINCT FROM u.display_name;
```

You need another query for each case of denormalization in your database. This is one reason to be conservative in how many places you denormalize data.

You may run these quality control queries manually, or configure a scheduler to run them automatically. As your collection of quality control grows, and they take longer as your database grows, it may take a long time to run all these queries.

Documenting Procedures and Policies

Other software developers will take over maintaining the Visage database and application. They need to know which tables contain denormalized data, why it was done, and what to do when there are discrepancies.

You need to create a reference document to help those engineers. Here's an example that shows notes for two denormalized columns. It includes enough information so that another developer can learn *why* the denormalized column was implemented. It also includes details of implementation that are known at the time, but would be lost and hard to rediscover later. In addition, identify the quality control (QC) that is used to monitor data integrity. These notes help any developer who needs to debug a problem. For project management, you might also include notes about the date it was first implemented and the number of a ticket in your work breakdown tool that has further discussion. Include the name of a developer to contact if there are any further questions.

```
Denormalized Column: post.author_display_name
Origin Column:       user.display_name
Optimizes Func:      PostDetail()
Sync Method:         Trigger, upd_denorm_user_name()
Sync Frequency:      Immediate
QC Script:           check-display-name.py
QC Frequency:        Daily from cron
Date Implemented:    2025-03-11
Reference Ticket:    DEV-0175
Contact:             @g.hopper

Denormalized Column: post.avg_rating
Origin Column:       rating.rating
Optimizes Func:      PostIndex()
Sync Method:         Cron, calc-rating.py
Sync Frequency:      Hourly from cron
QC Script:           (none yet)
Date Implemented:    2025-06-24
Reference Ticket:    DEV-0204
Contact:             @m.hamilton
```

This is just an example. Your notes might include different fields. You can use whatever you think serves best to help your teammates avoid stumbling around in the dark when they need to debug or modify the code or database. The point is to keep some notes in a central place (like a project wiki or a cloud document), make sure every team member knows where to find them, and keep them up to date as you implement new cases of denormalization.

Once your quality control queries reveal some discrepancies in the data, you must decide what to do about them.

For example, if a row in post has an avg_rating that doesn't match when you recalculate the average from the set of rows in the rating table, should you recalculate and replace the aggregated value in post? Or should you correct one or more of the ratings so that their average works out to the stored average, or investigate to see if a bug occurred such that a rating was added or deleted without recalculating the stored average?

Sometimes you have a policy about how to handle a given discrepancy. In the case of the average rating, you might choose a policy to always prefer the rows in rating as the correct values and to recalculate and replace the stored average. In another case, the policy may require a thorough investigation of any discrepancy. You could even choose policies on a case-by-case basis within the same project, for each denormalized column.

Document carefully, so you and other teammates know how to maintain the denormalized data.

Keeping an Exit Strategy

At some point, you may have felt enough pain and extra work of maintaining denormalized data such that you'd really like to undo these cases and rely only on normalized data. Is this a possibility? Remember that it was done originally to simplify or optimize certain SQL queries. If those SQL queries are still important in your application, then you probably need to maintain the denormalized data.

But what if the original SQL query that the denormalization was meant to support is no longer important? It may not even be in the code anymore. Software often changes, and the code that required the denormalization may have been refactored or replaced.

This is why you kept the notes. You can quickly research whether the function named is still part of the application. If it's not, then it's time to remove the complexity of that case of denormalization. You should notify the person named as a contact to make sure they agree.

If you and your team hadn't kept those notes, it might be difficult or impossible to know if it's safe to retire a given denormalized column, and then you'd have to maintain it indefinitely for no benefit.

Every kind of optimization improves a given query, but at the expense of other queries.

Mini-Antipattern: Query Snipers

What can you do about runaway queries?

Queries can run for an unexpectedly long time. If you haven't created the right indexes to optimize the query, or if the query's conditions force examining too many rows, it could take orders of magnitude longer than you can afford to wait. Even a query that normally runs well can suddenly perform poorly because the database server is under extreme load.

Some SQL products include a feature to terminate a query if it exceeds a specified run time. For example, PostgreSQL has the option `statement_timeout`. You set this option to an integer, measured in milliseconds. If the query runs longer than this value, it ends without returning a result, and the client gets the following error instead:

```
START TRANSACTION;
SET LOCAL statement_timeout = 5000;
SELECT ...query that takes longer than 5000 milliseconds...
...
ERROR:  canceling statement due to statement timeout
```

If this feature is effective at blocking queries that run too long, then why not set it all the time? It's possible to set it in the PostgreSQL options file, so every session starts with a cap on query execution time. However, it's hard to choose the right value for that cap.

If you set the global limit too high, this fails to limit runaway queries before they overtax the server, or the delay may still be long enough to annoy users.

If you set the global limit too low, this fails to account for occasional queries that need to be allowed to run to completion. Some queries are important because the application can't proceed without the needed information, or because the query is in fact an `INSERT`, `UPDATE`, or `DELETE` that must execute successfully.

If the query times out, the application may be forced to retry it until either it succeeds or else its repeated failure creates a serious incident.

The appropriate statement timeout is different for each query because each query has a different threshold for what seems to be too long.

The best practice is to allow queries unlimited time as a default. If this is a problem for a specific case, then spend some effort to investigate why the query is taking too long. Optimize the query if you can. For instance, most problematic queries just need an index to help reduce the examined rows.

If you can't optimize the query any further, there still could be a solution. Designing a new query that gets the results using a different approach could be the solution. The database server might need to be upgraded. The data stored in the database might have grown too large and need to be archived.

You would never implement an arbitrary time limit on any method of code in your application. The same is true of SQL queries.

It's not practical to set a one-size-fits-all limit for the duration of all queries.

An ill workman quarrels with his tools.

John Ray

CHAPTER 8

NoSQL: The Grass Is Always Greener on the Other Side

"Something is wrong with Eris," I said, as I showed my screen to the site reliability engineer who designed the dashboard that tracked our datacenter infrastructure. For some reason, he had named the dashboard *Eris* after the Greek goddess of discord. "It seems to show a server in the Western region, but the server is part of a network that's only in the Eastern region. I logged into the server and checked its IP address, and it's definitely in the Eastern network. Why is it listed in the Western region in this dashboard?"

The engineer, Anthony, looked up from his keyboard and shrugged. "Well, that's part of the grand mystery of software, sometimes it says things you don't understand," he said carelessly.

"That's not an answer," I said. "You designed the data model for our infrastructure database; where did you store a server's region?"

"With the server record," Anthony answered.

"But that means a server's region might be different from the region of the network it's in," I reminded him. "The server has to belong to a network, and a given server has to be in the same region as its network. So the data model should not store the region with the server—it should get that from the network record. That's basic data normalization."

Anthony thought for a moment, then he looked like he had gotten an idea. "I'm going to migrate the data from PostgreSQL to MongoDB," Anthony announced.

"How will that correct the data conflict?" I asked.

"MongoDB doesn't need data normalization," Anthony said with a wave of his hand. "It's a document database, not a relational database. Rules of normalization don't apply."

"But data anomalies still apply," I reminded him. "When the dashboard shows false information, we could waste time on server operations, or we could destabilize the company by rebooting a server that we think isn't in the live region. This is a bug we need to fix."

Anthony shook his head. "It's not a bug if there's no rule it's violating," he insisted. "Rules are the way things were done in the past. Document databases are about freedom. Document databases are the future!" He turned back to his keyboard. To him, the conversation was over.

Suddenly, I thought naming the application after the Greek goddess of discord was a good choice.

Objective: Relief from the Challenges of SQL

The next component of the Visage application you need is a reporting system for marketing to track usage of the social media site. Marketing wants to know which posts are getting the most engagement, measured by a combination of the number of views, ratings, and comments. The prototype SQL query for this report aggregates counts from the `comment` and `rating` tables, and joins those to the respective `post` where the `view_count` is stored.

NoSQL/engagement.sql

```
SELECT p.post_id, (p.view_count
    + COALESCE(c.comment_count,0)
    + COALESCE(r.rating_count,0)) AS engagement
FROM post AS p
LEFT OUTER JOIN (
  SELECT post_id, COUNT(*) as comment_count
  FROM comment
  GROUP BY post_id
) AS c USING (post_id)
LEFT OUTER JOIN (
  SELECT post_id, COUNT(*) AS rating_count
  FROM rating
  GROUP BY post_id
) AS r USING (post_id)
ORDER BY engagement DESC
LIMIT 10;
```

Some software developers find this kind of SQL query to be a chore. For them, the theory and practice of SQL and relational database modeling are constraining and tedious. They would rather jump into writing their application code, and not spend time refining their data model before they can write their first line of code that uses the database.

You can imagine a wish list for a database that supports easier development:

- No time-consuming data model analysis
- Simpler query syntax and semantics
- Scalability by distributing data over multiple database instances
- High performance (of course)

Developers naturally look for a new technology that has these advantages.

Antipattern: Switching to NoSQL Is Easy

There's a category of database management software called *NoSQL*, which claims the benefits you're looking for. However, many products claim to be NoSQL. You need to know which one is best for your engagement report project, so you ask your project manager to introduce you to some developers who have used different NoSQL solutions.

Attempt #1: A Humongous Problem

You are assigned to work with Mark. He's a big fan of MongoDB.

Mark dives into the Visage code and adds lines to open a connection to MongoDB. He also develops a data migration tool to copy data from the `post`, `comment`, and `rating` tables in Visage's PostgreSQL database into equivalent *collections* in MongoDB.

He explains that collections in MongoDB are more or less analogous to tables in an SQL database. A collection in MongoDB contains a number of *documents*. Documents are more flexible than rows in SQL because for a document, you don't have to declare field names or types in advance. By simply referencing fields of the collection, Mark can load data into them, like the keys of a `dict` in Python. A document in the collection isn't required to have distinct fields from other documents in the same collection.

Mark works on the engagement report query for MongoDB for a while, and when he returns, he shows you the following code:

NoSQL/anti/engagement-mongodb.py
```
from pymongo import MongoClient

client = MongoClient("localhost")

visage = client["visage"]
```

```
results = visage.post.aggregate([
    {
        "$lookup": {
            "from": "comment",
            "localField": "id",
            "foreignField": "post_id",
            "pipeline": [
                { "$group": { "_id": None, "count": { "$count": {} } } }
            ],
            "as": "comment"
        }
    },
    {
        "$lookup": {
            "from": "rating",
            "localField": "id",
            "foreignField": "post_id",
            "pipeline": [
                { "$group": { "_id": None, "count": { "$count": {} } } }
            ],
            "as": "rating"
        }
    },
    {
        "$project": {
            "id": 1,
            "title": 1,
            "user_id": 1,
            "engagement": {
                "$add": [
                    { "$ifNull": [ "$view_count", 0 ] },
                    { "$ifNull": [ "$comment[0].count", 0 ] },
                    { "$ifNull": [ "$rating[0].count", 0 ] }
                ]
            }
        }
    },
    { "$sort": { "engagement": -1 } },
    { "$limit": 10 }
])

for f in results:
    print(f)

client.close()
```

The first thing you notice about this MongoDB query is that it can hardly be called simpler or easier to read than the SQL prototype you had originally proposed. In fact, it's significantly longer. It's not written in a query language as you know it—it's written as an intricate nested data structure, using Python lists and dicts. At first glance, it's hard to tell the difference between query operators, field names, and literal values. It's going to take a while of studying MongoDB's reference documentation to understand this code.

There's also a more urgent problem: as you help Mark test the report, you find that it's producing the wrong result. The numbers don't match the results you got from the prototype SQL query. You and Mark inspect the MongoDB collection carefully, and eventually you realize that halfway through Mark's data migration, he changed his mind about some of the field names. In about half the documents of the `post` collection, he stored the count of views in a field named `views`. In the other half, he stored that value in a field named `view_count`. His query is only referencing the field `view_count`, so it's only counting views for half of the posts.

Now, you and Mark have to choose one of the following fixes. Either redesign the query to reference fields by both their old name and new name, and combine the results somehow, or clean up the data to make the field names consistent. Both of these alternatives would put this work behind schedule and make the project more complex. If you had developed any other queries against this collection, you'd also have to make sure that changing the field names wouldn't cause those queries to get the wrong results.

Having put the project behind schedule, Mark gets reassigned.

Attempt #2: Don't Say I Didn't Warn You

You're assigned to work with another engineer, Cleo. You explain the problem MongoDB had with the field names, and she nods. "MongoDB is too flexible," she concludes. "Let's use a NoSQL product that has better support for defining consistent field names."

You thought MongoDB *was* NoSQL.

Cleo smiles as she explains in a kind of yes-but-no tone. "MongoDB is one NoSQL product, but there are many different databases that qualify as NoSQL. It's like saying you're using a vehicle that is 'NoMotorcycle'—that could be a car, or a boat, or a hang glider, or a skateboard, or a train..." She's enumerating these by counting them on her fingers, and she can tell you get the point. "Obviously, all of them are not motorcycles, and they are all used for travel. But that's the only thing they have in common. They're different from a motorcycle, and they're different from each other, too."

She proposes to use an open source NoSQL product called Cassandra. In Cassandra, you can define tables with more concrete columns, similar to

SQL. Cassandra has its own declarative query language called *CQL*, instead of queries coded as a lengthy nested data structure.

Cleo manages to copy data into three tables she defines in Cassandra for post, comment, and rating. Then she writes the following new code for the engagement report:

NoSQL/anti/engagement-cassandra.py

```
from cassandra.cluster import Cluster
from cassandra.query import dict_factory
from operator import itemgetter

cluster = Cluster()
session = cluster.connect()
session.set_keyspace("visage")

results = session.execute("SELECT post_id, view_count FROM post")

post_unsorted = []

for post in results:
    post_id = post.post_id

    comment_count = session.execute("""
        SELECT COUNT(*) AS count FROM comment
        WHERE post_id=%s
        ALLOW FILTERING""",
        [post_id])

    rating_count = session.execute("""
        SELECT COUNT(*) AS count FROM rating
        WHERE post_id=%s
        ALLOW FILTERING""",
        [post_id])

    engagement = post.view_count + comment_count[0][0] + rating_count[0][0]

    post_unsorted.append({"post_id": post_id, "engagement": engagement})

post_sorted = sorted(post_unsorted, key=itemgetter("engagement"), reverse=True)

print(post_sorted[:10])
```

This looks a lot simpler than the previous MongoDB attempt. One CQL query produces a list of posts. Then, a Python loop counts related comments and ratings, one post at a time. Add the three elements together with a simple addition expression in Python. Finally, sort the results using Python's standard sorted() function. The first 10 items in the sorted Python list are returned as a slice of the sorted list.

However, during testing, Cassandra has a different problem. The more records you store in post, the worse the performance gets. This is because the number of queries required for the comments and ratings increases in direct proportion to the number of iterations of the loop. If you had thousands of posts, this code would run thousands of queries. Since each query adds a little overhead, soon the code is suffering from bad performance, even if the queries are individually quick.

When you ask Cleo to explain why she wrote her code this way, she explains, "Cassandra doesn't support joins or subqueries; each query can reference only one table. To get counts from the other tables, I chose to do that in the loop."

Reconsidering the Mission

At this point, it seems like both attempts to use NoSQL have surprising disadvantages that make them no better than using SQL. It hasn't panned out that NoSQL products make software development simpler or more efficient. On the contrary, both attempts seemed to make the project harder. Can the truth about NoSQL be that it is *worse* than SQL?

No, not really—but we'll see shortly that both Mark and Cleo could have used NoSQL solutions in better ways.

How to Recognize the Antipattern

- "MongoDB is a *web-scale* database that doesn't use SQL or joins, so it's high-performance."

  It's unrealistic to claim that any technology product is the best in every application, and this quote is based on the false assumption that an SQL query with joins can't be optimized.

- "How do I write this SQL query in NoSQL?"

  Sometimes, there isn't a one-to-one equivalent query because to use NoSQL properly, you'll be better off redesigning your data structure from scratch. Trying to rewrite a given SQL query for NoSQL probably indicates that you haven't taken the time to do this.

- "NoSQL is better than SQL for CMS systems."

  This oversimplifies the variety of queries in an application. An individual query might be easier or more efficient implemented with one type of database or the other, but it's too much of a generalization to apply that to a broad category or vertical. This quote is not only about CMS systems; you might hear people make the same claim about any other kind of application.

Legitimate Uses of the Antipattern

Using a NoSQL solution is a perfectly legitimate option. Every tool or technology can serve you well when you design your data and code for it.

The antipattern is using NoSQL as a drop-in surrogate for SQL, trying to replace each table and each SQL query one-for-one with their NoSQL equivalent. You'll fail to utilize the NoSQL product's strengths, and the result likely will be worse than using either SQL or NoSQL, if done properly. We'll see examples in the next section.

The marketing of some NoSQL products has promoted the fact that they don't require you to spend time meticulously designing tables and schema. It feels like you're more productive because you can begin writing your application code without so much analysis. But it still requires work and analysis to develop NoSQL-based applications that are efficient. The difference is that instead of spending time analyzing the schema, you spend time analyzing queries.

Your queries are what guide your NoSQL database design.

If you embrace that part of using NoSQL, you'll be more successful. If you skip all analysis, then you'll quickly get into trouble, and you might think that NoSQL is at fault.

Solution: Match Your Queries to Your NoSQL Models

The important principle to make the best use of NoSQL is to let your application's queries drive the design of your data structure.

In a relational database, you should design tables according to the rules of normalization. This prevents data anomalies, and the tables are prepared for a wide variety of queries against the same data, even if they aren't optimized for any specific query.

But NoSQL has no rules of normalization. You don't get the benefit of preventing data anomalies or the flexibility of running a variety of queries, but you might gain better optimization for one particular query. If that query is one your application needs to be most efficient, then it's a good design. In this way, you should think of designing a NoSQL database as similar to designing a denormalized SQL database, as we saw in Chapter 7, Premature Denormalization, on page 67.

Let's look at examples of how Mark and Cleo might have redesigned the data for MongoDB and Cassandra. The way you store data for NoSQL is often quite different from how you store data for SQL. These aren't the only possible solutions, or even necessarily the best—they're just better than the attempts shown in the Antipattern section.

Fixing MongoDB

What could the collection look like in MongoDB? Instead of storing related documents in three separate collections, we could make the comments and ratings part of the related post collection. MongoDB document data structures support nested data structures.

NoSQL/soln/mongodb-post.json

```
{
  "id": 1234,
  "title": "Who's On First?",
  "user_id": 3,
  "view_count": 2902909,
  "comments": [
    {
      "id": 1, "user_id": 1,
      "comment": "Well, let's see, we have on the St Louis team, Who's on
        first, What's on second, I Don't Know is on third..."
    },
    {
      "id": 2, "user_id": 2, "in_reply_to": 1,
      "comment": "That's what I want to find out."
    }
  ],
  "ratings": [
    { "user_id": 3, "rating": 2 },
    { "user_id": 4, "rating": 4 }
  ]
}
```

This allows your query to skip the $lookup operations. Instead, you can count comments and ratings by using the $size operator to get the length of these nested arrays.

NoSQL/soln/engagement-mongodb.py

```
from pymongo import MongoClient

client = MongoClient("localhost")

visage = client["visage"]

results = visage.post.aggregate([
    {
        "$project": {
```

```
                "id": 1,
                "title": 1,
                "user_id": 1,
                "engagement": {
                    "$add": [
                        { "$ifNull": [ "$view_count", 0 ] },
                        { "$size": { "$ifNull": [ "$comments", [] ] } },
                        { "$size": { "$ifNull": [ "$ratings", [] ] } }
                    ]
                }
            }
        },
        { "$sort": { "engagement": -1 } },
        { "$limit": 10 }
])

for f in results:
    print(f)

client.close()
```

This is a lot shorter and easier to read than Mark's first attempt.

Fixing Cassandra

What could the table look like in Cassandra? Since a Cassandra query can query only one table, store all the data you need for the report in one table—including the post itself, and subsequent views, comments, and ratings. The table may become very long because each row is one kind of *event* that happened to a post. That's okay, and it will make the query easier.

NoSQL/soln/cassandra-event-table.cql

```
CREATE TABLE post_event (
    post_id INT,
    id UUID,
    event_type TEXT,
    event_dt TIMESTAMP,
    user_id INT,
    content TEXT,
    rating INT,
    PRIMARY KEY (post_id, id)
)
```

Some columns, such as event_type and event_dt, are relevant to all events. Other columns are relevant only to certain events, like content and rating. Cassandra is designed to work well with tables that have a lot of columns, many of which are NULL. The following shows example data for the post_event table.

post_event

post_id	event_type	event_dt	user_id	content	rating
1234	POST	1938-03-24	1	Who's On First?	NULL
1234	COMMENT	1938-03-24	2	Are you the manager?	NULL
1234	COMMENT	1938-03-24	1	Yes.	NULL
1234	COMMENT	1938-03-24	2	You gonna be the coach too?	NULL
1234	COMMENT	1938-03-24	1	Yes.	NULL
1234	COMMENT	1938-03-24	2	And you don't know the fellows' names?	NULL
1234	COMMENT	1938-03-24	1	Well I should.	NULL
1234	COMMENT	1938-03-24	2	Well then who's on first?	NULL
1234	COMMENT	1938-03-24	1	Yes.	NULL
1234	VIEW	1938-03-24	42	NULL	NULL
1234	VIEW	1938-03-24	43	NULL	NULL
1234	VIEW	1938-03-24	44	NULL	NULL
1234	VIEW	1938-03-24	45	NULL	NULL
1234	RATING	1938-03-26	3	NULL	2
1234	RATING	1938-03-27	4	NULL	4
1234	RATING	1938-03-28	5	NULL	5

•
•
•

Now, you don't need to run separate queries to get aggregate counts. Just count the rows, grouping by the post_id to get a subtotal of events per post.

NoSQL/soln/engagement-cassandra.py

```
from cassandra.cluster import Cluster
from cassandra.query import dict_factory
from operator import itemgetter

cluster = Cluster()
session = cluster.connect()
session.set_keyspace("visage")

results = session.execute("""
    SELECT post_id, COUNT(*) AS engagement
    FROM post_event
    WHERE event_type IN ('COMMENT', 'VIEW', 'RATING')
    GROUP BY post_id
    ALLOW FILTERING""")

for post in results:
    print(post)
```

By tailoring the table design to the query you need to run the engagement report, you simplify development and avoid the overhead of running so many queries in the loop.

Choosing Tradeoffs and Priorities

You can't develop a single code architecture that optimizes for everything. This is practically the definition of optimization—to improve one usage pattern at the expense of other usage patterns. Since we're talking about databases, that really means different queries. It's a much simpler goal to use the solution you choose to optimize one query, after you acknowledge that other queries won't be optimized to the same degree. They may still perform adequately given the performance tolerance of your application.

Analyze your application's needs and decide which usage is the highest priority. Then choose SQL or one of the types of NoSQL, based on how well it supports the functions you most need to optimize in your application. The alternative, if your project has mandated use of a technology, is to change your application design to take advantage of the strengths of the chosen database.

No technology used naively gives you performance or scalability. You get that from your application architecture.

Mini-Antipattern: N+1 Queries

In the previous Cassandra example, we saw that the developer wrote code to run CQL queries in a loop, to fetch related data from a second table. This is necessary when using Cassandra because CQL doesn't support joins.

The same antipattern can happen in an application that uses SQL if you decide not to use JOIN in a query.

In the following example, first, one query fetches all the posts. Then, in a loop, one query for each post fetches the comments related to that post:

NoSQL/anti/nplusone.py

```
import psycopg2
import psycopg2.extras

conn = psycopg2.connect("dbname='visage' host='localhost'")

with conn.cursor(cursor_factory=psycopg2.extras.RealDictCursor) as cur:

    cur.execute("""SELECT post_id, view_count FROM post""")
    posts = cur.fetchall()

    for post in posts:
        cur.execute("""
            SELECT comment_id, comment_text, in_reply_to,
                user_id, created_at
```

```
        FROM comment
        WHERE post_id = %(post_id)s
        """, post)
    comments = cur.fetchall()
```

Why should we consider this an antipattern? Is running two queries really that much of a problem?

If it were just two queries, perhaps it would be okay. But the risk is that the first query on the post table might return a lot of rows. What if there are a hundred posts? Ten thousand? A million?

Each additional query adds a small amount of overhead. It might only be a few milliseconds per query, but if you multiply that by a thousand, you can see that the overhead adds up and may cause your request to be delayed by whole seconds.

It might seem quick enough while you're developing and testing the code, but after your code has been in production for a few weeks or months, and the number of posts grows, it becomes more costly. What seemed to work well with a small amount of testing data gradually gets slower and slower.

Using a JOIN reduces the overhead by turning N+1 queries into a single query.

Fallacies do not cease to be fallacies because they become fashions.

G. K. Chesterton

CHAPTER 9

JSON: Matryoshka Dolls

"Welcome to the Visage reporting team," your new manager, Siobhán, says. She is smiling, but seems subdued.

"Thanks," you say brightly. "What can you tell me about the other members of the team?"

"I'm afraid it's just you," she replies, her voice going low. "You're the fourth replacement developer this year. Ever since Hugh created the *database within a database*."

"Who is Hugh?" you ask. "And what is the database within a database?"

"Hugh was a brilliant developer ... but a little erratic," she explains. "Early in the Visage project, feature requirements weren't all quite settled, so Hugh came up with a way to store data in flexible tables."

You look confused.

She goes on, "Instead of using conventional tables and columns, he created tables that could adapt to the product manager's priorities using JSON. We can store any data we need, as requirements change. But now, it's a bit difficult to maintain reporting queries. Some of them have stymied several developers, and they asked to move to another part of the company. I'm so glad you're here; we have a backlog of unfinished reporting requests."

"Can I ask Hugh some questions?" you ask.

Siobhán sighs. "Hugh took a job at a hot startup company last year. He's no longer here. But I think he left notes about his database design, I'll put them on the file server for you."

Objective: Unlimited Flexibility

As you develop an application, not every feature is known at the time you create the database. You learn new things about the data entities and attributes needed as you go, or the product manager makes a decision to add features that weren't included in the original plan. From time to time, you need to add columns to tables, change data types of existing columns, or rename columns. These kinds of changes are done with ALTER TABLE in SQL.

At first, Hugh tried to follow the standard practice of altering tables every time a requirement changed. This felt like a bottleneck for the rapidly evolving project. Once a table contains data, changing its design means you must block work while it is locked and being restructured. Even changing column names or data types required code revision because any SQL query that referenced the columns needed to be changed to match. Altering tables in an SQL database that is in use is like reforming a concrete foundation with a house on top of it.

To avoid this awkwardness, Hugh found a way to make the tables flexible and dynamic so that they can adapt to new features as the application develops. His objective was to design tables once and never need to use ALTER TABLE.

But there was a problem ...

Antipattern: Semi-Structured Data in a Relational Database

Hugh decided to store data in JSON format. This met his need for a flexible data model, but in some ways it made working with his tables more complex and less efficient. Let's take a closer look at what Hugh used JSON for, and how its conveniences come at a cost.

Implementing with JSON

Traditionally, each column of a row in an SQL table stores one scalar value, like a string, number, or datetime. This way, it's easy to guarantee a column stores the same type on every row, and you can write a query to read individual values.

Modern SQL databases also support the JSON data type, which allows a column to store multiple values on a given row. JSON is a notation for a type of semi-structured data. You don't define a fixed schema for the elements within the JSON column as you do when you define columns of a conventional

SQL table. One JSON column can contain not just a single string, number, or datetime, but it also may contain a *document*, which is an array, or an object (a set of key-value pairs, like a Python dict), or it can be nested further. It can be an array of objects, or an object where each value is an array or an object. In theory, these structures can have unlimited depth.

This is what Hugh meant when he wrote that his design was a database within a database. JSON can be like a Matryoshka doll—a set of hollow wooden dolls, each with a smaller doll inside it. Unless you're careful, you can end up creating complex, nested data structures that are hard to use.

Since Hugh was using PostgreSQL, he used the `JSONB` data type for semi-structured data. The following code shows a few examples of how Hugh stored JSON documents. All three are just strings to SQL, but within each string, the JSON notation represents different structures: for example, an array, an object, or an array of objects.

JSON/anti/initialize.sql

```
ALTER TABLE post
  ADD COLUMN IF NOT EXISTS tag_ids JSONB,
  ADD COLUMN IF NOT EXISTS metadata JSONB,
  ADD COLUMN IF NOT EXISTS revisions JSONB;

UPDATE post
SET tag_ids = '[1,2,3]',
    metadata = '{
        "date_created": "2025-05-01",
        "date_updated": "2025-06-01"
      }',
    revisions = '[
      {"revision": 2, "edit_date": "2025-05-10", "editor": "Jules"},
      {"revision": 3, "edit_date": "2025-05-12", "editor": "Mike"},
      {"revision": 4, "edit_date": "2025-05-15", "editor": "Sharon"}
    ]'
WHERE post_id = 1234;
```

The flexibility of JSON allowed Hugh to store a document, potentially with a different structure, on each subsequent row in this table. He could use any structure he needed, adding or omitting object keys as the data required, or adding further levels of nested structures for multivalued attributes.

Document-oriented data have structure, in that you can refer to discrete elements within the document, but they don't have a fixed schema. In a conventional relational data model, every row of a given table has the same set of attributes, one per column. In a given column, all the values are of the same type and are in the same domain. Whereas in a semi-structured data model, a document stored on one row doesn't necessarily have the same

> **JSON and JSONB in PostgreSQL**
>
> PostgreSQL implements two related data types: JSON and JSONB.
>
> The former stores a JSON document as literal text, as if you stored a JSON document in a TEXT column. The JSON document must be parsed every time you query it, whereas JSONB parses the JSON document once, when you insert it, and then stores an internal structure that makes it quicker to modify. JSONB also supports indexing, and some of the built-in functions in PostgreSQL work only with JSONB.
>
> Usually, JSONB is preferred over the JSON data type in PostgreSQL.

attributes as a document stored on another row in the same column of the same table.

The semi-structured model is like using a NoSQL database. In fact, it can be a hybrid approach. Hugh defined some fixed columns as required by SQL, but also defined a column in the same table to store a document, effectively extending each row with a dynamic set of new attributes.

At first, the JSON feature seems like exactly what Hugh wanted. However, this amount of flexibility comes with several complications, which you now have to support. Let's take a look at some of these.

Querying JSON Is Harder, Not Easier

While it seems easier to store semi-structured data, querying those data requires new methods. SQL databases that support JSON also need new built-in functions or expressions for searching or modifying JSON. Before moving data into JSON documents, you should consider how complex your queries will become.

Let's look at several examples of queries needed in the Visage application. It quickly becomes clear that we have to think about query logic in new ways when we work with semi-structured data.

Searching for a Key/Value Pair

You're designing a screen to display posts that were created on June 1, and the date created is stored in a JSON column. You could use the traditional pattern-matching operator LIKE:

JSON/anti/json-search.sql

```
SELECT * FROM post
WHERE metadata::text LIKE '%2025-06-01%';
```

But this incorrectly finds a post that was updated on June 1 instead of created on June 1. The JSON document contains the date you want, but not for the date_created key. Using a broad text search is likely to produce false matches.

To solve this, you need to learn to use built-in JSON functions or operators. Fortunately, PostgreSQL has a rich set of special functions for unpacking such documents, such as the JSON extraction operator ->> to get a string value for a named key. The following example shows a more specific search (in this case, it correctly finds no match, instead of a false match that returns the wrong row):

JSON/anti/json-search.sql

```
SELECT * FROM post
WHERE metadata->>'date_created' = '2025-06-01';
```

In another part of Visage, you query a more complex structure, searching for a post that was revised by "Mike" on May 12. You can use the JSON_TABLE() function to expand some kinds of JSON structures into rows and columns, as if they had been stored in a normalized table. This allows you to refer to fields of the same object because they are returned as columns on the same row of a table that is the result of the expansion by the JSON_TABLE() function.

JSON/anti/json-table.sql

```
SELECT post.* FROM post
CROSS JOIN JSON_TABLE(revisions, '$[*]' COLUMNS (
    revision INT PATH '$.revision',
    edit_date DATE PATH '$.edit_date',
    editor TEXT PATH '$.editor'
  )) AS r
WHERE r.editor = 'Mike' AND r.edit_date = '2025-05-12';
```

This is a lot of code. It would have been quite simple SQL if you had created a new table revision to store revisions in normal rows and columns to begin with. That might have looked like the following:

JSON/soln/normal-revision.sql

```
SELECT post.* FROM post
JOIN revision AS r USING (post_id)
WHERE r.editor = 'Mike' AND r.edit_date = '2025-05-12';
```

Using Custom Attributes

JSON_TABLE() works best if your JSON document is an array of objects, and the objects have a similar set of fields. If your JSON document is more complex or has inconsistent fields, it gets progressively harder. In another table, you discover that Hugh stored arbitrary attributes for user accounts not as an array of objects, but instead as a JSON object with a variety of keys.

He must have added a column to the table with an alteration like the following example:

JSON/anti/json-custom-attributes.sql

```
ALTER TABLE "user"
  ADD COLUMN IF NOT EXISTS properties JSONB;
```

Any time a new attribute was needed, he could just make up a new key and add it to the new document. You can even see cases where he misspelled a key that had been used before. These updates looked like the following:

JSON/anti/json-custom-attributes.sql

```
UPDATE "user"
SET properties = '{
    "haircolor": "blonde",
    "birthday": "November 23",
    "hobby": "harpist"
  }'
WHERE user_id = 5;

UPDATE "user"
SET properties = '{
    "haircolo": "black",
    "birthday": "October 2",
    "alias": "Rufus T. Firefly"
  }'
WHERE user_id = 3;
```

In this case, the JSONB_EACH_TEXT() function returns a dynamic set of rows, one for each key it finds in the JSON object argument. That key is a string that you can use to extract a corresponding sub-document from the revisions, and then further extract each field from the sub-document.

JSON/anti/json-custom-attributes.sql

```
SELECT u.user_id, u.real_name, j.* FROM "user" AS u
CROSS JOIN jsonb_each_text(properties) j(key, value)
WHERE u.user_id IN (3, 5);
```

The output looks like the following:

user_id	real_name	key	value
5	Harpo Marx	hobby	harpist
5	Harpo Marx	birthday	November 23
5	Harpo Marx	hairColo	blonde
3	Groucho Marx	alias	Rufus T. Firefly
3	Groucho Marx	birthday	October 2
3	Groucho Marx	hairColor	black

This almost gets what you want, but the custom attributes are returned one per row, and the concrete columns are repeated. What if you want the custom attributes stored in the properties JSON document to be returned as columns? Remember, in Chapter 4, Dynamic Pivot, on page 35, you saw that an SQL query must have a fixed set of columns. A query can't produce a variable number of columns depending on the data it reads during execution.

PostgreSQL has a function, JSONB_POPULATE_RECORD(), which produces multiple columns in the query result, but it still requires that you specify a record type with a fixed set of columns. If the JSON object has fields that don't match the column names in this record type (even misspellings), they're ignored.

JSON/anti/json-custom-attributes.sql
```
CREATE TYPE myrowtype AS (hobby TEXT, birthday TEXT,
  haircolor TEXT, alias TEXT);

SELECT u.user_id, u.real_name, j.* FROM "user" AS u
CROSS JOIN jsonb_populate_record(null::myrowtype, properties) j
WHERE u.user_id IN (3, 5);
```

user_id	real_name	hobby	birthday	haircolor	alias
5	Harpo Marx	harpist	November 23	blonde	
3	Groucho Marx		October 2		Rufus T. Firefly

Even in PostgreSQL, a query can't populate columns of unknown number and type.

Ever More Complexity

As you investigate further in the Visage application, you notice a row that has a different metadata document than others you've seen:

JSON/anti/json-extended-metadata.json
```
{
  "date_created": "2025-05-01",
  "date_updated": "2025-06-01",
  "references": [
    {
      "type": "book",
      "title": "SQL Antipatterns, Volume 1",
      "authors": [ "Bill Karwin" ],
      "date": "2022"
    },{
      "type": "blog",
      "url": "https://karwin.com/blog/index.php/2009/05/21/eav-fail/"
    }
  ]
}
```

This is an undocumented structure, with more keys and more nested levels. It opens up new potential queries that might be needed. For instance, you might expect to be asked to search for posts that reference more than one book by a given author, or a resource more than ten years old.

Still, there's no guarantee this is the last example of semi-structured data with unexpected structure. JSON is so flexible that you can't predict whether other rows exist now or will be inserted in the future.

As you consider each case of JSON documents with greater complexity, a pattern emerges: you have to learn new ways of querying the document for each new level of nesting or other difference in the structure. SQL may be hard enough, but relational tables are fundamentally just rows of columns. JSON is bound to be more complex, and there's no limit to how much more complex it can be.

Changing Documents Retroactively

You've seen how the structure of a document supports the queries you run against those documents. As queries in your application are added or changed, the JSON structure may need to change. In a conventional relational table, when you use ALTER TABLE to change columns, this is applied retroactively to all rows in that table. But with JSON documents, you don't execute ALTER TABLE. You just start inserting new documents with a different structure. This applies to new data, but old data is still stored in the old structure.

As you inspect Hugh's code in Visage, you find cases where the application interprets JSON documents differently depending on when they were created. In the following example, it appears that the original created_at column became a field in the metadata JSON object, first called created_at. Then, about two weeks later, he apparently changed the JSON key to date_created.

Hugh decided to write three queries with UNION, limiting each query to a specific date range. Hugh knew the dates when the document structure was changed, and he hard-coded these dates in his query. This way, the value will be extracted from the row correctly, depending on the date.

JSON/anti/json-document-versions.py

```
import psycopg2

conn = psycopg2.connect("dbname='visage' host='localhost'")

with conn.cursor() as cur:

    cur.execute("""
      SELECT post_id, created_at
      FROM post
```

```
    WHERE post_id = %(post_id)s
      AND created_at < '2021-06-14'
    UNION
    SELECT post_id, (metadata->>'created_at')::timestamp AS created_at
    FROM post
    WHERE post_id = %(post_id)s
      AND created_at BETWEEN '2021-06-14' AND '2021-07-02'
    UNION
    SELECT post_id, (metadata->>'date_created')::timestamp AS created_at
    FROM post
    WHERE post_id = %(post_id)s
      AND created_at > '2021-07-02' OR created_at IS NULL
""", {'post_id': 1234})

print(cur.fetchall())
```

But it's not clear that this query is truly correct. How do you know Hugh got the dates right? Are there any other structures stored in the table that this query doesn't account for? How many other queries elsewhere in the application have similar conditional queries? You get a sinking feeling as you consider these questions, and you realize that to answer them, you'll have to inspect a lot of data and code manually.

This is going to be a long, painful project.

Calculating Storage

Storage is almost always a premium resource. Databases tend to grow rapidly, and eventually they threaten to fill up the available storage space. This risk is multiplied when data are stored in JSON or JSONB documents instead of normal rows and columns.

In a conventional SQL table, the column names are metadata that is stored only once in the table definition, regardless of the number of rows. But in JSON, since documents can have objects with varying keys, the keys must be stored on every row. This increases the storage, even if the data values are the same in both a normal table and a table using JSON. If the keys are very long strings, this overhead is even greater.

To prove this, you can create some test tables to store data in normal rows and columns, and compare that to the same data stored in JSON or JSONB:

JSON/anti/json-table-size.sql

```
CREATE TABLE post_size_test_1 (
  post_id BIGSERIAL PRIMARY KEY,
  post_title TEXT NOT NULL,
  post_text TEXT NOT NULL,
  user_id BIGINT NOT NULL DEFAULT 0,
  created_at TIMESTAMP NOT NULL DEFAULT CURRENT_TIMESTAMP,
```

```
  updated_at TIMESTAMP NOT NULL DEFAULT CURRENT_TIMESTAMP
);

CREATE TABLE post_size_test_2 (
  post_id BIGSERIAL PRIMARY KEY,
  attributes JSON
);

CREATE TABLE post_size_test_3 (
  post_id BIGSERIAL PRIMARY KEY,
  attributes JSONB
);

CREATE TABLE post_size_test_4 (
  post_id BIGSERIAL PRIMARY KEY,
  attributes JSONB
);
```

The first table has normal columns. Fill this table with 1 million rows of random text:

JSON/anti/json-table-size.sql

```
INSERT INTO post_size_test_1 (post_title, post_text)
  SELECT
    RPAD(GENERATE_SERIES::VARCHAR, 40, MD5(RANDOM()::TEXT)) AS post_title,
    RPAD(GENERATE_SERIES::VARCHAR, 16*1024, MD5(RANDOM()::TEXT)) AS post_text
  FROM GENERATE_SERIES(1, 1000000);
```

The second table uses the JSON type, which stores the text of the document. The third table uses the JSONB type, since you'd like to know if it uses more or less storage for the pre-parsed version of a JSON document. Copy the rows (minus the primary key post_id) of the first table into the JSON documents:

JSON/anti/json-table-size.sql

```
INSERT INTO post_size_test_2 (post_id, attributes)
  SELECT post_id, TO_JSONB(p) - 'post_id' FROM post_size_test_1 AS p;

INSERT INTO post_size_test_3 (post_id, attributes)
  SELECT post_id, TO_JSONB(p) - 'post_id' FROM post_size_test_1 AS p;
```

Finally, try to increase the key length of the elements in the JSON object. You can do this by copying the fields into a JSON document one at a time, with a key string repeated 10 times:

JSON/anti/json-table-size.sql

```
INSERT INTO post_size_test_4 (post_id, attributes)
  SELECT post_id,
    JSON_OBJECT(
      REPEAT('post_title', 10): post_title,
      REPEAT('post_text', 10): post_title,
      REPEAT('user_id', 10): user_id,
      REPEAT('created_at', 10): created_at,
```

```
    REPEAT('updated_at', 10): updated_at
  )
FROM post_size_test_1;
```

Then, use PostgreSQL catalog tables to measure the table sizes:

JSON/anti/json-table-size.sql

```
SELECT table_schema, table_name,
  pg_size_pretty(table_bytes) AS table,
  pg_size_pretty(index_bytes) AS index,
  pg_size_pretty(total_bytes) AS total
FROM (
  SELECT *, total_bytes - index_bytes
    - COALESCE(toast_bytes, 0) AS table_bytes
  FROM (
    SELECT
      c.oid,
      nspname AS table_schema,
      relname AS table_name,
      pg_total_relation_size(c.oid) AS total_bytes,
      pg_indexes_size(c.oid) AS index_bytes,
      pg_total_relation_size(reltoastrelid) AS toast_bytes
    FROM pg_class c
    LEFT JOIN pg_namespace n ON n.oid = c.relnamespace
    WHERE relkind = 'r'
  ) a
) a
WHERE table_schema = 'public' AND table_name LIKE 'post_size_test%'
ORDER BY table_name;
```

As you can see in the figure at the top of the next page, the table with normal columns uses 361MB. The table storing JSON takes 433MB, and JSONB is slightly higher, at 456MB. If the object keys are very long, it's much worse—732MB.

These results may vary depending on how many elements you put in JSON documents, which data types you use, and how long the keys and values are. But in general, the more data you store in JSON, the more overhead there is. Your storage space will run out faster. If you need to be mindful about using storage economically, think twice before using JSON or JSONB.

How to Recognize the Antipattern

- "The product team didn't decide on required features, so I just started coding the application using dynamic fields."

  Developers under schedule pressure may choose to create a "flexible" data model to make it easy to change it later.

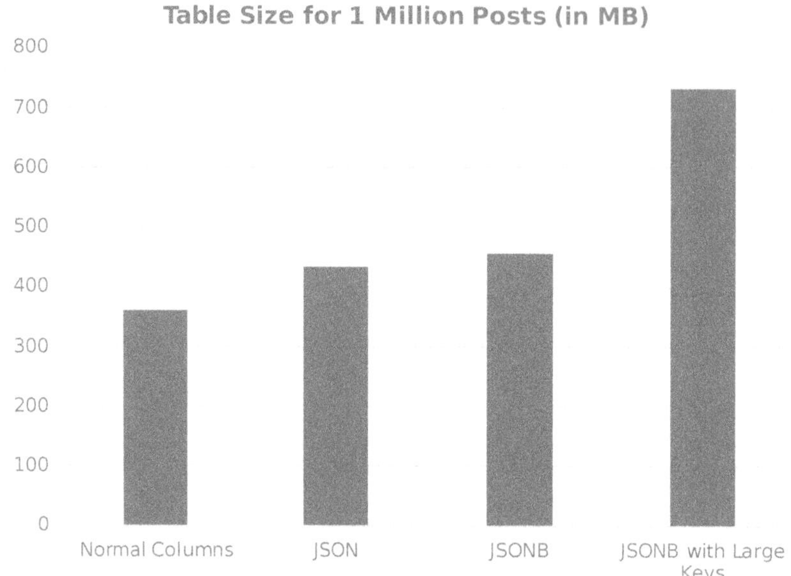

- "Why did I use JSON columns? Because it's a new feature in the database and I wanted to try it."

  It's surprisingly common for developers to choose a new technology for practice or experimentation, instead of choosing proven technology.

- "Can you help me write an SQL report query against JSON? I don't know how to do that. I inherited this database from the previous developer, who decided for some reason to use JSON, and I can't change it now."

  An unfortunate reality is that developers sometimes get stuck maintaining code they didn't develop, using technology they aren't familiar with.

Legitimate Uses of the Antipattern

Like any specialized tool, JSON should be used in specialized circumstances.

The best use of JSON is when a table represents sparse or unpredictable attributes. A good example is a retail product catalog for a large shopping site with frequent changes to product inventory. For example, books have attributes like page count, binding, ISBN number, or publisher. These

When Did Each Brand of SQL Database First Support JSON?

The ISO SQL:2016 standard defined syntax for JSON in response to the rise of NoSQL databases that stored JSON documents.

Current versions of all popular RDBMS support it. Each brand of SQL database implemented the JSON type and built-in functions at different times. The following list shows the first version of the most popular SQL brands that supported a JSON data type.

- PostgreSQL 9.2 (2012)
- Informix 12.10.0 (2013)
- Oracle 12c Release 1 (2013)
- MySQL 5.7 (2015)
- SQLite 3.9.0, as an extension (2015)
- Microsoft SQL Server 2016
- IBM DB2 11.1 (2016)
- SQLite 3.38.0, built in (2022)

Some of these were years before SQL standardized the JSON features, so some brands had to invent their own nonstandard syntax, and each brand that did this didn't necessarily implement it the same way other brands did. Each brand also supports different built-in functions for working with JSON data.

If you are working with JSON, make sure you study the documentation for the brand and exact version you are using because some implementations added features and functions gradually over several versions.

If you're developing a software product that must support more than one brand of SQL database, it's even more challenging. The best solution is the same as writing so-called "portable SQL" with respect to any other features, which is to use the Adapter pattern to implement brand-specific code in a class or function that implements a common interface, making it possible to swap for another implementation.

attributes aren't relevant to other product types like shoes, electronics, or decorations, and those products have their own unique attributes. It would be a burden to require a new table with fixed columns for every one of thousands of product types, so it makes sense to use semi-structured data for product-specific attributes.

In some cases, it might be worth using JSON as a form of denormalization. Storing a collection in an array makes sense if you treat the collection as an attribute to be fetched whole. The same caveats you read about in Chapter 7, Premature Denormalization, on page 67 apply to this case; it depends on the queries you need to run and whether you can commit to maintaining the fragile structure of the data.

You can also use JSON format as a "black box"—a place to store semi-structured data that the application needs, without using SQL to reference the elements within the JSON document. Your only reference to the JSON in SQL would be to INSERT a document, then later SELECT or UPDATE the whole document. Any further use of the JSON would be in application code.

Solution: Be Mindful and Moderate About Flexibility

The danger of JSON is the result of its limitless flexibility. A relational database works best with a fixed structure, so you can employ constraints and simplify your queries. The way to use JSON successfully is to use it sparingly, and only for cases where the normal approach really can't do a task.

Choosing Normal Tables

As you saw in the antipattern section of this chapter, searching fields in JSON documents is frequently harder than searching normal columns. Given the choice of how to store a given attribute, it makes sense to prefer to use a normal column if your queries reference that attribute in searching or sorting.

It's a code smell if a query references any JSON column in any clause of a SELECT query after the select-list. That is, using normal columns is better for joining, searching in the WHERE clause, grouping, and ORDER BY. Once the query has produced a set of rows that match the criteria, manipulating JSON documents in expressions in the select-list is relatively harmless.

Another code smell is when your JSON document is a virtual row set. For example, the revisions document Hugh created, where it's just an array of objects with identical keys, should have been stored as normal rows in a dependent table.

Likewise, a multivalued attribute, like the tag_ids array, is easier to implement as a many-to-many intersection table. Instead of packing and unpacking an array, you can insert and delete individual rows.

Checking Against a JSON Schema

Few uses of JSON need the unlimited flexibility of documents and sub-documents. Usually, the semi-structured data follows patterns, even if there is some variation within limits. For these cases, you can enforce limits by validating the document against a *JSON Schema*. A JSON Schema is a notation that describes the types of structures allowed.

For example, MySQL 8.0.17 supports a built-in function JSON_SCHEMA_VALID() which returns true if the JSON document complies with a given JSON Schema.

You can use that function to validate JSON content before inserting, using a trigger or a CHECK constraint, as in the following example for MySQL:

JSON/soln/json-schema-mysql.sql
```
CREATE TABLE post (
  post_id SERIAL,
  post_title TEXT NOT NULL,
  post_text TEXT NOT NULL,
  user_id BIGINT NOT NULL,
  revisions JSON CHECK(JSON_SCHEMA_VALID('{
      "$schema": "http://json-schema.org/draft-04/schema#",
      "title": "List of changes to a post",
      "type":"array",
      "items": {
        "type": "object",
        "properties": {
          "revision": {
            "type": "number"
          },
          "edit_date": {
            "type": "string"
          },
          "editor": {
            "type": "string"
          }
        },
        "required": ["revision", "edit_date", "editor"],
        "additionalProperties": false
      }
    }', revisions))
);
```

This JSON Schema describes the revisions document, which must be an array of objects. The objects must have properties revision, edit_date, and editor. These properties are required in each object of the array, and no additional properties are allowed.

You can read more about the JSON Schema notation at json-schema.org.[1]

PostgreSQL doesn't have built-in support, but there are several community extensions to implement it. The current most popular is pg_jsonschema,[2] developed by the company Supabase, Inc.

Oracle 23c also supports built-in features to support JSON Schema validation.[3]

1. https://json-schema.org/
2. https://github.com/supabase/pg_jsonschema
3. https://docs.oracle.com/en/database/oracle//oracle-database/23/adjsn/json-schema.html

Microsoft SQL Server, IBM DB2, and Informix don't support JSON Schema validation at the time of this writing.

Now, it may be more clear what Hugh meant by the database within a database. It's not simply that JSON can have nested arrays and objects. Hugh meant that JSON effectively implements a structure within the conventional SQL structure. A given application may assume elements within the document have a structure, either implicitly or by using JSON Schema to make the structure more stable.

The more you do this, the more it looks like a set of normal tables with rows and columns. Using JSON Schema, you end up having done just as much work describing the structure, but the syntax is less readable than SQL data definition language.

Working with JSON in a Legacy Project

You may find yourself maintaining an application that someone else designed, like the example in this chapter of Hugh's database within a database. In fact, this is more common than working on brand new projects. According to *Facts and Fallacies of Software Engineering [Gla92]*, software in maintenance accounts for about 60 percent of software development work on average.

If you find yourself in that situation, it pays to spend some time studying the application and the unique ways it uses flexible data structures.

Even if the application and database don't enforce a JSON Schema, that's at least a standard notation you can use to document the structure of documents you find in the database. If the project documentation doesn't include that reference, make it your responsibility to create it. This means you read the existing code and inspect documents stored in the database.

To prepare for application enhancement requests that involve querying data stored in JSON documents, you should familiarize yourself with the built-in functions and operators the current database provides. For example, for PostgreSQL, you would read the reference documentation for JSON functions and operators.[4] Make sure you study the documentation for the version of database software your project uses. If your project uses an older version, then reading about functions in the current version might mislead you into trying to use a function that isn't implemented.

4. https://www.postgresql.org/docs/current/functions-json.html

Working with JSON in a New Project

If you are working on a new greenfield project, it's up to you to design the database to minimize the complexity and overhead of JSON. Use it when necessary, if there's no efficient way to implement normal tables with rows and columns to meet your requirements. But resist the temptation to use JSON for reasons of convenience.

If your motivation to use JSON is to avoid the cost of using `ALTER TABLE`, then investigate options for concurrent changes. For MySQL, free community tools such as `pt-online-schema-change`[5] have been used to run alterations with no downtime on busy production instances at many companies, including financial applications. For PostgreSQL, you can try similar experimental tools such as Reshape[6] or `pg-osc`.[7] Removing the pain of `ALTER TABLE` makes it a lot easier to use normal rows and columns, but still handle changes.

If you have product managers or customers who have a hard time sticking to decisions about features, this is actually a more difficult problem because it isn't a technology problem—it's a communication problem. You can do your best to accommodate shifting requirements, changing the code and database structure, but the indecision can eventually be greater than your ability to keep up. In that case, you can try strategies such as the following:

Communicate Your Estimates

When you are asked to make a change, it's a good practice first to respond positively that you will do the work, but then make it clear how much time it will take, and that it may require changes to the project's schedule. It's a good idea to have these conversations with the product manager in private to avoid embarrassing them. Be calm and respectful, but stick to your estimates.

Negotiate

If you can think of an alternative software design that doesn't require altering existing tables, propose that. Another way to negotiate is to agree to implement a change for a later phase of the project, so the current phase can stay on schedule. Ask about the priority of the change, and if it can be postponed.

5. https://docs.percona.com/percona-toolkit/pt-online-schema-change.html
6. https://github.com/fabianlindfors/reshape
7. https://github.com/shayonj/pg-osc

Develop Prototypes

Some product managers can't tell you what they want, and they can't envision the application even if they read a design document. But they can tell you what's wrong with an application once they can see it and try it. For these kinds of managers, you have to rapidly develop a prototype application and let them test it and give feedback. The prototypes are only for the purpose of helping discuss the goal for the project. They aren't supposed to become the production software. It's more like a clay model a sculptor uses for experimentation before starting to work on their art piece in a final material like stone, wood, or metal.

These strategies aren't specifically about database design—they can work for any software changes.

Making Sense of the Conflict

Many features of SQL rely on all the rows of a table having the same fixed set of columns. But semi-structured data like JSON encourage a more fluid structure, where any row may effectively have a different set of attributes. It's hard to manage these two paradigms seamlessly. You can use JSON with SQL if you're careful, but like denormalization, you should use it sparingly and be mindful of the hidden costs.

With great flexibility comes great responsibility.

Mini-Antipattern: Quotes for All Occasions

The use of quote symbols in SQL causes some confusion for programmers, and when JSON is added to SQL, it gets even more complicated.

The single quote is the delimiter for string literals. Strings always need this type of quote.

The double quote is the delimiter for identifiers, such as table names or column names. Identifiers don't need this type of delimiter if they comply with simple identifier format. Use delimiters if the identifier contains special characters like spaces or punctuation or non-ASCII characters, or if it conflicts with an SQL reserved keyword, or if you want it to be case-sensitive.

The following example shows the use of both quotes. The `user` table must be delimited because `user` is an SQL reserved keyword:

```
SELECT * FROM "user" WHERE display_name = 'groucho';
```

Sometimes programmers mix up the types of quotes, and it causes errors. In the following example, column names are incorrectly delimited with single quotes, which causes a syntax error:

```
INSERT INTO post ('post_title', 'post_text', 'user_id') VALUES ...
```

```
ERROR:  syntax error at or near "'post_title'"
LINE 1: INSERT INTO post ('post_title', 'post_text', 'user_id') VALU...
```

SQL never uses smart quotes as delimiters. It's a good idea to use a code editor that doesn't insert them. In the following example, SQL thinks the column name contains literal smart quotes, which doesn't match the actual name:

```
INSERT INTO post (“post_title”, “post_text”, “user_id”) VALUES ...
```

```
ERROR:  column "“post_title”" of relation "post" does not exist
LINE 1: INSERT INTO post (“post_title”, “post_text”, “user_id”) VALU...
```

If you need to include a literal single quote in a string (for example, an apostrophe), then escape the character so it isn't interpreted as the end delimiter. The SQL standard says to do this by using two adjacent quote characters, but most SQL products also allow escaping with a backslash:

```
SELECT * FROM "user" WHERE display_name = 'O''Hare';
```

```
SELECT * FROM "user" WHERE display_name = 'O\'Hare';
```

If you need to include a literal double quote in an identifier (this is rare but technically allowed), then escape the character in a similar way. For example, if the table's name were `odd"name`—with a literal double quote character in the middle of the table name—you would delimit the identifier in one of the following ways:

```
SELECT * FROM "odd""name" WHERE display_name = 'groucho';
```

```
SELECT * FROM "odd\"name" WHERE display_name = 'groucho';
```

In SQL, a JSON document is simply a string, so the whole document must be delimited in single quotes like any other string. Within that string, double quotes delimit JSON keys and string values:

```
UPDATE post
SET metadata = '{
        "date_created": "2025-05-01",
        "date_updated": "2025-06-01"
      }'
WHERE post_id = 1234;
```

If the JSON document contains a literal single quote, then you must escape it for SQL as you would in any other string.

If a JSON key or string value contains a literal double quote, SQL doesn't mind. A double quote inside a single-quoted string doesn't conflict with SQL string literal delimiters. But JSON requires you to escape each literal double quote with a backslash, as in the following example:

```
UPDATE post
SET metadata = '{
        "signature": "Ernest \"Papa\" Hemingway"
      }'
WHERE post_id = 1234;
```

You need to pay attention carefully to quotes in any programming language, but it's especially tricky when using JSON in SQL.

For to win one hundred victories in one hundred battles is not the acme of skill. To subdue the enemy without fighting is the acme of skill.

Sun Tzu, The Art of War

CHAPTER 10

Cacheless Transactions

"We've got a problem," your manager, Paul, whispers as he approaches your desk, looking tired. "The customer survey results say that the Visage site is way too slow."

You open your mouth to object, but Paul holds up a hand. "I know what you're going to say," he offers. "You've been doing everything you can to optimize the SQL queries—and you've done a great job!" he adds the last part quickly. "All the screens on the site meet their performance goals, and then some. Except ..."

Your eyes get wide. "Except ... the home page?"

Paul nods once.

Your optimization work didn't include the home page because it hadn't been finished. The product manager, Terry, was still deciding what to show on the home page. So, the code was developed quickly at the very end of the project, literally hours before the big public launch. You never had a chance to review the code, nor was there any time to change it anyway.

Paul goes on. "The home page is, obviously, a user's first impression of Visage. Even though all the other pages are fine, if the home page loads too slowly, users lose interest. And it's loading *much* too slowly. Reports from the access logs show that over half the visitors to the site click away before the page fully loads."

"So what do you want me to do?" you ask.

"Pair with the developers and fix it ASAP," Paul says. "Do anything you need to. Treat this as top priority."

Objective: A Magic Trick to Improve Performance

Performance optimization is always desirable, but in this case, it's critical. Your objective is to optimize the database queries until the home page of Visage loads reliably in under 10 milliseconds. Unfortunately, the current page loads in about 10 seconds (10,000 milliseconds). You need to reduce this by three orders of magnitude.

You're also told that Terry won't change his mind about the dynamic content that appears on the home page. Your assignment is to optimize the page load time without removing anything.

The development team thinks the items on the home page taking the most time are the following:

- A count of recently active users
- Four of the latest posts
- The most recent public company blog post

Everything else on the home page is static, so you don't have to worry about that. The developers are buzzing among themselves about compressing JavaScript or putting graphics on a content delivery network, but you'll leave those tasks to them.

Antipattern: The Performance Vanishing Act

It would be nice if you could wave a magic wand to make the execution time of these queries simply disappear. There are no such magic wands in real life, but you might find a trick that works just as well. First, you need to understand the queries that the home page currently runs. You can't study code in a meeting; you have to open up the code files and read them.

It'll save time if you pair with someone familiar with the code to help explain it. Rafael has been working on the code most recently, so he offers to work on it with you. He shows you the following Python Flask code for the home page, which looks like it simply runs three SQL queries and passes the results to a web template:

Caching/anti/app.py

```
from flask import Flask, render_template
import psycopg2
import psycopg2.extras

app = Flask(__name__)

@app.route("/", methods=['GET'])
```

```
def homepage():
    with psycopg2.connect("dbname='visage' host='localhost'") as conn:

        cur = conn.cursor(cursor_factory=psycopg2.extras.RealDictCursor)

        #  Most recent public company blog post.
        cur.execute("""
            SELECT post_id, post_title,
                LEFT(post_text, 100) AS post_text_short
            FROM post JOIN "user" USING (user_id)
            WHERE user_type_id = 1
            ORDER BY updated_at DESC LIMIT 1
        """)
        latest_blog_post = cur.fetchone()

        # A count of recently active users.
        cur.execute("""
            SELECT COUNT(DISTINCT user_id) AS count
            FROM (
                SELECT user_id FROM comment
                WHERE created_at > NOW() - INTERVAL '1' DAY
                UNION
                SELECT user_id FROM post
                WHERE updated_at > NOW() - INTERVAL '1' DAY
            ) AS u;
        """)
        recent_user_count = cur.fetchone()

        #  Four of the latest posts.
        cur.execute("""
            SELECT post_id, post_title,
                LEFT(post_text, 100) AS post_text_short
            FROM post
            ORDER BY updated_at DESC LIMIT 4
        """)
        recent_posts = cur.fetchall()

    return render_template('home.html',
                           latest_blog_post=latest_blog_post,
                           recent_user_count=recent_user_count,
                           recent_posts=recent_posts)

if __name__ == '__main__':
    app.run()
```

Then, he shows you the web presentation template that displays the home page:

Caching/anti/templates/home.html

```
<!DOCTYPE html>
<html>
<head><title>Visage Home</title></head>
<body>
  <h1>Visage</h1>
```

```
  <hr>

  <h2>Message from HQ</h2>
  <h3>{{latest_blog_post['post_title']}}</h3>
  <p>{{latest_blog_post['post_text_short']}}...</p>

  <h2>Recent active users: {{recent_user_count['count']}}</h2>

  <h2>Recent posts</h2>
  {% for post in recent_posts %}
    <h3>{{post['post_title']}}</h3>
    <p>{{post['post_text_short']}}...</p>
  {% endfor %}

</body>
</html>
```

Neither of these code files is very complex, but the problem is that the SQL queries take too long.

Rafael tells you the team has already done everything they could think of to optimize the queries on this page. They avoided non-sargable queries and made sure joins, search conditions, and sorting use indexes where possible. They tried denormalization, but found that changing the tables read by these queries harmed performance in other parts of Visage. They even upgraded the database server as much as they could afford. After all these efforts, the 10-second page load time is the best they could achieve.

Just as you're running out of ideas about how to squeeze any more performance out of these queries, Rafael says in despair, "If only we didn't have to run these SQL queries on every page view."

You suddenly realize that he's inadvertently described the solution. There is a way to do the impossible—to display query results *without* running a query every time.

The solution, as we'll see shortly, is to use a *cache*.

How to Recognize the Antipattern

- "Do you know any way we can optimize this SQL query any further? We've tried *everything*."

  They've used common methods to improve performance, and they're getting desperate because it's still not enough to meet their goal.

- "I'm submitting a proposal for an emergency budget to upgrade the database server. We need more horsepower."

It's possible the server is underpowered, but an upgrade is sometimes just a very expensive way to avoid stepping back and reconsidering the software design.

- "It's absolutely required that every query return 100 percent current data."

  This statement is likely not true, but the speaker is making it a strict requirement because they haven't thought about which queries could return slightly delayed data.

Legitimate Uses of the Antipattern

Should your takeaway from this chapter be that querying data is an antipattern? Not at all.

It's fine to run an SQL query on demand during a web request. In a database where data is changing, we naturally want to display results with the most recent changes, and running queries is how we do that.

In any application, different subsets of data change more frequently than others. Some cases of viewing data are more strict in that they must show the latest data. Some applications even stream live updates to the user's view in real time.

Optimize the query as well as you can, if that query must be executed every time the user requests the view. If you have already optimized the query, then it might help performance to run the database software on a more powerful server with faster processors or more RAM. Finally, set expectations so users know how quickly the query can return results.

The antipattern is repeating a query *unnecessarily*. You don't need to run the query if your code already has a copy of the result from executing that query earlier, and the data hasn't changed in the database since that query. Or, even if the data has changed in the database, it could be unnecessary to run the query if the previous result is still accurate enough for a given application view.

Solution: Use Sleight of Hand

Reading data from a cache service is a solution to improve the performance of the home page by orders of magnitude. When a user browses to the Visage home page, the request is handled by code that reads data from the cache, which is much faster than running the SQL queries.

This works well because reading data from the cache skips the overhead of all the other things an SQL engine does: parsing SQL, checking privileges, optimizing the query, scanning through large amounts of data, aggregating

Numbers Everyone Should Know

In 2010, Jeff Dean, the chief scientist at Google, gave a lecture at Stanford about "Building Software Systems at Google and Lessons Learned."[a] One of the lessons he shared was how important it was for software designers to be fluent with the cost in latency of computer operations and to be able to use those figures to estimate the total latency of any given approach the software developer may be thinking of using.

He showed a table of typical low-level operations in the CPU, I/O, or networking, all measured in nanoseconds (ns).

L1 cache reference	0.5 ns
Branch mispredict	5 ns
L2 cache reference	7 ns
Mutex lock/unlock	25 ns
Main memory reference	100 ns
Compress 1 KB w/cheap compression algorithm	3,000 ns
Send 2 KB over 1 Gbps network	20,000 ns
Read 1 MB sequentially from memory	250,000 ns
Round trip within same datacenter	500,000 ns
Disk seek	10,000,000 ns
Read 1 MB sequentially from disk	20,000,000 ns
Send packet CA->Netherlands->CA	150,000,000 ns

The point is not that everyone needs to memorize these specific numbers, but that they should be aware that different operations take orders of magnitude more or less time, and they should prefer to design software with economy. For example, these numbers show that one read from a slow storage device takes about the same time as 200,000 memory reads; keeping this in mind as you design code should help you to choose better trade-offs.

The specific numbers in Dean's presentation were based on his experience with computer systems in 2010 or before. Computer systems improve every year, so these figures have changed and will continue to change. You should measure the performance of the platform you use, ideally by testing it yourself.

Few projects run at the scale of Google, but keeping these principles in mind will improve the performance of software systems at any scale.

---

a. https://www.youtube.com/watch?v=modXC5IWTJI

results into rows, and returning the results to the client. Furthermore, the data examined by the query may require reading from persistent storage, which is much slower than memory. The difference depends on the query, but in some cases, it's thousands of times faster to read from cache.

Adding Cache to the Code

Opening a cache resource in your application looks a little similar to opening a database resource. Use a specific client package; for the Visage application, you could use flask_caching.Cache. This package supports multiple cache service technologies. In the example, the resource configuration names RedisCache as the type of service (this code is tested with Valkey 9.0,[1] an open source fork of Redis).

Caching/soln/app-cache.py

```
from flask_caching import Cache

cache = Cache(app, config={"CACHE_TYPE": "RedisCache"})
```

That's it—after opening this resource, you can write code to *get* (read) or *set* (write) values in the cache. This cache service is basically like a Python dict structure, holding values indexed by a key. It stores this set of key-value pairs in dynamic memory, so it's very fast. When you try to get a key that has no value stored, it returns None. When you set a key that's already in the cache, the new value replaces the existing value stored.

For each SQL query, add code that first tries to read the data from the cache. If the data is present in the cache, then use it and skip the query. Otherwise, run the SQL query and save the result to the cache so the next request may find it.

Caching/soln/app-cache.py

```
# Most recent public company blog post.
latest_blog_post = cache.get("latest_blog_post")
if latest_blog_post is None:
    cur.execute("""
        SELECT post_id, post_title,
            LEFT(post_text, 100) AS post_text_short
        FROM post JOIN "user" USING (user_id)
        WHERE user_type_id = 1
        ORDER BY updated_at DESC LIMIT 1
    """)
    latest_blog_post = cur.fetchone()
    cache.set("latest_blog_post", latest_blog_post)
```

Write a similar code block for the other two queries.

This way, most of the requests are able to use the data from the cache. Only the first request must run the SQL query. You could even run that request yourself, priming the cache, so none of your users have to experience a slow response.

1. https://valkey.io/

Can You Do Better?

Showing the prototype to Terry, the first thing he sees is the initial request to prime the cache. That request takes 10.01 seconds, according to your web profiler. Subsequent requests take between 0.006 and 0.008 seconds—achieving your goal of under 10 milliseconds.

But Terry still isn't happy. "Why was it slow the first time?" he asks. "I don't want any users to have that experience. Can you make the first one quick, too?"

Back to the drawing board ...

You can improve the design by reading from cache on *every* request for the home page. The following code shows how the home page request handler becomes much simpler:

Caching/soln/app-cache-prime.py
```
@app.route("/", methods=['GET'])
def homepage():

    # Most recent public company blog post.
    latest_blog_post = cache.get("latest_blog_post") or {}

    # A count of recently active users.
    recent_user_count = cache.get("recent_user_count") or {'count':0}

    #  Four of the latest posts.
    recent_posts = cache.get("recent_posts") or []

    return render_template('home.html',
                           latest_blog_post=latest_blog_post,
                           recent_user_count=recent_user_count,
                           recent_posts=recent_posts)
```

You'll have to make sure that the cached data is primed. There are several ways to do this.

In the case of the count of active users, create a scheduled job to refresh the cache. A standalone Python script like the following can do this:

Caching/soln/update-user-count.py
```
#!python

import psycopg2
import redis

with psycopg2.connect("dbname='visage' host='localhost'") as conn:

    with conn.cursor() as cur:

        cur.execute("""
            SELECT COUNT(DISTINCT user_id) AS count
            FROM (
```

```
            SELECT user_id FROM comment
            WHERE created_at > NOW() - INTERVAL '1' DAY
            UNION
            SELECT user_id FROM post
            WHERE updated_at > NOW() - INTERVAL '1' DAY
        ) AS u;
    """)
    recent_user_count = cur.fetchone()[0]

    with redis.Redis() as cache:
        cache.set("recent_user_count", recent_user_count)
```

Then, use cron to run the script every 30 minutes.

Caching/soln/update-user-count.crontab

```
*/30 * * * * /usr/local/bin/update-user-count.py
```

This solution works because it's not necessary to be precise or perfectly current. Anyone interested in this figure can use the cached value, even if it takes up to 30 minutes to get the latest count. Some degree of tolerance for delayed or approximate results is common—more common than we often assume.

Another method of keeping a cache up to date is to save the value in the cache when it changes. In the case of the set of four latest posts, you assume that users visit the Visage site to read posts more frequently than new posts are written. So, it's a good trade-off to update the set only when someone writes a new post. You don't even need to run a query to scan the post table. Just add the new post to the list, and pop the oldest of the four posts in the cache off the list. In the following code that handles the post submission form, the new content is inserted into the post table, and in the same request, the cache entry is updated with a modified list, so it always has the most recent four posts.

Caching/soln/app-cache-prime.py

```
@app.route("/post_submit", methods=['POST'])
def post_submit():

    with psycopg2.connect("dbname='visage' host='localhost'") as conn:

        with conn.cursor() as cur:

            # Insert new post to database
            cur.execute("""
                INSERT INTO post (post_title, post_text, user_id)
                VALUES (%(post_title)s, %(post_text)s, %(user_id)s)
                RETURNING post_id
            """,
                        {'post_title': request.form['post_title'],
                         'post_text': request.form['post_text'],
                         'user_id': 1})
            new_post_id = cur.fetchone()[0]
```

```
        # Update cache to add the new post just created,
        # and hold no more than 4 posts.
        # Use Lock to prevent race conditions.
        with lock:
            recent_posts = cache.get("recent_posts") or []
            recent_posts = recent_posts[-3:]

            new_post = {
                "post_id": new_post_id,
                "post_title": request.form['post_title'],
                "post_text_short": request.form['post_text'][:100]
            }

            recent_posts.append(new_post)
            cache.set("recent_posts", recent_posts)

    return redirect('/')
```

Using techniques like these, the home page (which is requested far more frequently) avoids the cost of running any SQL query, and it's optimized as much as possible for every user.

Cache Invalidation

Perhaps the trickiest aspect of using a cache is *cache invalidation*, which is the way you decide that an entry in the cache needs to be replaced with more current data. Phil Karlton, a senior software engineer at Netscape, made the following observation in the 1990s:

> There are only two hard things in computer science: cache invalidation and naming things.

This is a hard thing because there's no single right or wrong answer. It's always a trade-off between refreshing the cached data as frequently as you need, versus minimizing the number of costly queries. It's up to you to make a choice on where you'll compromise between those two priorities. You'll find that you need to evaluate every situation independently. Every application has different needs, and even individual queries in a given application need to be handled differently.

Why Don't We Always Use Cache?

If reading from a cache is so much faster than an SQL database, wouldn't it make sense to stop using a database and store data only in the cache? That would maximize performance and eliminate the complex code to maintain two copies of the data.

A major downside of using a cache is that dynamic memory (RAM) is not persistent. The data stored in cache are lost if the cache process exits, just like any other in-memory variables or buffers that belong to that process. Some cache services, like Redis or Valkey, can optionally save their contents to persistent storage at intervals. But that's still not *durable* (see Appendix 1, ACID Transactions, on page 197 for more on durability).

This means what you store in a cache shouldn't be the only copy of that data. It should be possible for you to reconstruct the contents of a cache from data stored persistently elsewhere, likely in an SQL database.

The second reason a cache-only architecture is impractical for most applications is that RAM has always been more expensive than equivalently sized storage. In 2023, the price of 1 terabyte of RAM was typically $1,088, whereas the same size solid-state storage was $26, and for rotational storage devices it was $11, according to the website Our World in Data: Historical Price of Computer Memory and Storage.[2] The size of your data likely grows faster than you can afford to purchase RAM to hold it.

Third, it varies by product, but typical cache servers are less sophisticated in terms of data management than an RDBMS. They don't have a way to organize data into respective tables in the manner of relational normal forms. They may have no query language besides *get* or *set* by key. They may have no strong authentication or access privilege controls. They may not support concurrent access to the data, so as the rate of client requests increases, they will have to queue up.

Giving Cache Some Credit

This chapter showed some examples of ways you can use a cache service to complement the database, but it only scratches the surface. We haven't covered everything you could know about using a cache, but we've seen that it's an important part of your application architecture.

If you want to go deeper, *The Art of Scalability, 2nd Edition [AF15]*, has a chapter on caching. *Designing Data-Intensive Applications, 2nd Edition [KR26]* is a great book on managing large data sets in general.

The most optimized SQL query is the one you don't have to run at all.

2. https://ourworldindata.org/grapher/historical-cost-of-computer-memory-and-storage

Mini-Antipattern: Query Caching

We saw how much caching the results of queries improves performance. This leads to the question: why not make *every* query result cached automatically?

The idea is that if your application requests the exact same query multiple times, the first request stores the rows of the result in a cache, and then returns the same rows the next time the query is requested. This avoids the time and cost of re-running the query. It's also transparent to the client application. You don't have to write any code to manage storing into and fetching from the cache yourself. Just send the query, and the SQL engine automatically returns the result from cache if it's available.

In fact, a few SQL brands have tried to implement features for transparent caching of query results. Oracle 11G introduced SQL result caching and client result caching. Azure Synapse Analytics and IBM Cubing Services in InfoSphere Warehouse also have query result caching features. MySQL had a query cache from version 4.0 through 5.7, but it has since been deprecated and removed from the product.

Why isn't this a more popular feature?

One problem is that not all queries can be cached. Consider the following query, which returns new posts that have been written in the past hour:

```
SELECT * FROM post WHERE created_at > CURRENT_TIMESTAMP - INTERVAL '1' HOUR;
```

If you run the exact same query an hour later, it should return a different result. Posts that were included in the result in the previous hour are now more than an hour old, so they shouldn't be included. Meanwhile, new posts may have been written, and these should be included in the result.

More generally, any query that includes a nondeterministic expression (like NOW() that returns a different value from moment to moment) is not eligible to be cached. Features for query result caching have rules to detect such queries and make exceptions to avoid caching their results inappropriately.

Another problem is support for concurrent queries. If the SQL engine uses a shared memory buffer for caching the query results, it has to restrict access to that buffer, so concurrent sessions don't overwrite each other's entries or read an entry that isn't valid. Queries that otherwise would have been able to execute in parallel must wait for each other. In the case of MySQL's query cache, the feature eventually became known for doing more harm than good, and it was removed.

A third problem is cache invalidation, which we know is always hard. When programmers manage cached data manually, they choose when to refresh the data. Each use of cached data may need the latest data, or may be more tolerant of slightly stale data. But an automatic query result cache doesn't have the knowledge to make that choice. The only safe way for it to work is to be the most strict, and invalidate cached data immediately if the underlying data in tables changes in any way. Precisely tracking which data updates should trigger the invalidation of specific cached query results is costly—which defeats the purpose of avoiding the cost of running the queries.

Optimization requires the programmer to make choices, like which cases are higher priority for their application, and what compromises they're willing to make. Features that attempt to be one-size-fits-all, or try to be transparent for the programmer, take away opportunities to make those choices.

The better approach is to optimize on a case-by-case basis.

Part III

Application Design Antipatterns

SQL is supposed to be used in the context of applications written in another language, such as C++, Java, PHP, Python, or Ruby. There are right ways and wrong ways to employ SQL in an application, and this part of the book describes some common blunders.

Insanity is doing the same thing over and over again and expecting different results.

Anonymous

CHAPTER 11

Polling: Are We There Yet?

Your pager suddenly begins blaring, which means one of the alerts on the database server has been triggered. Checking the infrastructure dashboard, you see that the query traffic has suddenly doubled, spiking to 35,000 queries per second. You didn't know it could go that high on this server.

"Did anyone deploy a code change that could increase the query rate?" you ask quickly in the developers' chatroom.

A few minutes pass. Finally, a curt reply appears from Stas, the most sullen and uncommunicative member of the developer team. "No code change."

"Well, someone changed something," you continue.

"I doubled the number of app instances," Stas writes.

The architecture of Visage has one main database instance, but 15 application servers—now 30 application servers—each running an instance of the same code. The applications handle the web requests in parallel, but they all connect to the same main database. This has worked well enough up until now, but every database has its limits.

"How did that double the rate of queries?" you ask. "I understand it increases the capacity for handling traffic, but it shouldn't cause an immediate doubling of query traffic. I'd expect it to increase gradually."

Stas responds only with an emoji of a man shrugging his shoulders.

You investigate the query logs of the database server, and discover that almost all of the queries are the same, something like the following:

```
SELECT * FROM post
WHERE updated_at > NOW() - INTERVAL '1' MINUTE
  AND notified_at IS NULL
```

This query is accounting for more than 97 percent of the load on the database—sometimes many instances of the query are running concurrently.

Why is one query being run a thousand times per second by every application instance?

Objective: Notify of Changes to Data

It's fruitless to get Stas to explain, but eventually, by digging through git commit logs and long-forgotten software design documents, you find out the purpose of the mysterious query.

When posts are written in an interactive website like Visage, users want to be notified. But as the number of users increases, sending notifications gets more costly. When a user saves a post, they don't want to wait for a progress bar while notifications are being sent. They just want to save their post quickly.

So, the developers of Visage decided to process notifications asynchronously. That way, the user saving their post immediately sees that it's successful, while the Visage back-end application begins sending notifications to other users about the new content.

Of course, the other part of this objective is that notifications are timely. The back-end code needs to know as quickly as possible when it's time to notify users, and it needs to scale up to send notifications to all users promptly.

That sets the stage for a number of problems.

Antipattern: Polling for Changes

As you read through the history of the code revisions, you piece together how earlier developers like Stas designed the back-end code to check for new posts, then notify users of the new content.

Back-End Code Version 1

The following is how the first version of this code looked:

Polling/anti/backend-polling-v1.py

```
while True:
    with conn:
        with conn.cursor() as cur:

            cur.execute("""
                SELECT post_id FROM post
                WHERE updated_at > NOW() - INTERVAL '1' MINUTE
                  AND notified_at IS NULL
            """)
```

```
        posts = cur.fetchall()

        for post in posts:
            post_id = post[0]

            process_notifications(post_id)

            cur.execute("""
                UPDATE post SET notified_at = NOW()
                WHERE post_id = %(post_id)s
            """, {'post_id': post_id})
```

It queries for posts for which it hasn't sent notifications (notified_at IS NULL), and for each one, calls a function which you can assume sends notifications to the users who want them. Then it updates notified_at to the current timestamp, so the next time it checks, it'll skip that post.

Once the notifications have been sent and the posts updated, it's time to check again, so the loop iterates to the top. This is called *polling* the database.

Now you see why the query you observed runs so frequently. Suppose the query itself is well optimized and takes only 10 milliseconds. The time for the loop code is negligible. So, even if no one is writing new posts in Visage, the loop checking for new posts will iterate as many as 100 times per second. It can't slow down because when someone eventually does write a new post, the requirement is to send out notifications with as little delay as possible.

Back-End Code Version 2

The next revision of the code is almost identical, except it adds a line to the end of the loop to sleep for 60 seconds, to delay before the next query runs. This limited the load caused by the queries checking for unprocessed posts.

Polling/anti/backend-polling-v2.py

```
time.sleep(60)
```

But the next day, the line was changed to a low duration:

```
time.sleep(1)
```

And then increased again:

```
time.sleep(10)
```

Finally, it was changed to a line that reads the sleep duration value from an environment variable. Subsequently, the duration could have been changed any number of times without changing the code.

```
if "VISAGE_CHECK_DELAY" in os.environ:
    time.sleep(int(os.environ["VISAGE_CHECK_DELAY"]))
```

What's going on? You imagine there must have been numerous discussions about the best value for the sleep duration. Querying too frequently caused a high load on the database. Querying too infrequently caused users to be delayed in getting their notifications. No value could solve both problems.

Back-End Code Version 3

There was a final change to the code. As the popularity of Visage kept increasing, more posts were written, and more users wanted to be notified. A single function looping over posts and sending notifications serially couldn't keep up. So, the code was refactored by adding three lines to the SQL query, so that multiple back-end threads could work in parallel:

Polling/anti/backend-polling-v3.py

```
while True:

    with conn:

        with conn.cursor() as cur:

            cur.execute("""
                SELECT post_id FROM post
                WHERE updated_at > NOW() - INTERVAL '1' MINUTE
                  AND notified_at IS NULL
                FOR NO KEY UPDATE
                SKIP LOCKED
                LIMIT 1
            """)

            post = cur.fetchone()

            if post is not None:
                post_id = post[0]

                process_notifications(post_id)

                cur.execute("""
                    UPDATE post SET notified_at = NOW()
                    WHERE post_id = %(post_id)s
                """, {'post_id': post_id})
```

The first query in the preceding code has the following additional clauses:

- The FOR NO KEY UPDATE clause means it locks rows that it examines. The NO KEY part is a specific feature of PostgreSQL that allows the insertion of child rows that reference the locked row. For example, another session inserting a new row in comment would have to wait if it references a row in post locked with FOR UPDATE, but it would not wait if the row in post were locked with FOR NO KEY UPDATE.

- The SKIP LOCKED clause means that if the query tries to examine a row and can't immediately lock it because it's already locked by another instance, the query will skip the row and move on to the next row that isn't locked. We can assume the skipped row is locked because another session is already working on it. This solution avoids any delay from lock-waits, while every row is handled by one session.
- The LIMIT 1 clause means the query stops examining rows after it successfully reads and locks one row.

This modified query allows multiple instances to run concurrently. Which instance reserves a given row doesn't matter; what matters is that no row is read by more than one instance. Together, this design is effectively like a *queue*, in that each row is processed once by one of the back-end instances. After sending notifications for the locked row, the code commits the transaction, and committing automatically releases the lock.

If new posts are being added faster than the back-end instances can keep up with, then more instances can be started. They're simply Python scripts, and any number of them can be run on a given application server. You find that the current application server starts 10 instances of the new post checker script.

Again, this explains why you saw the query run so frequently, and why you sometimes saw many of the same query running concurrently. As more and more back-end instances are added to handle the traffic, they add more database sessions running the same query. Each server is configured to run 10 such instances, and Stas deployed 15 additional application servers. Now there's a total of 300 back-end instances over 30 servers, each running a loop to check repeatedly for new posts. The default delay in the loop is zero, so every one of the instances is looping as fast as it can.

Even if the query is well optimized, it's no longer a mystery why it accounts for 97 percent of the query traffic.

You still have the problem of how to reduce that load because the high traffic at this level is consuming so much processing power on the database server that it's degrading performance for all queries—including the remaining 3 percent of queries which serve the other functionality for Visage.

Shortly, you'll see how you can make notifications happen in a timely way, without using polling queries that overload the database.

How to Recognize the Antipattern

- "Why is the query load causing the server to melt down?"

  Even a powerful database server has a limit to the query throughput. Costly queries or a high volume of queries can exceed that limit.

- "How much delay is okay after an event before the back-end runs? Is five minutes too long?"

  A question like this might be heard from a developer who tries to compromise on latency.

Legitimate Uses of the Antipattern

When notification isn't real-time, but only on demand, then the application can check for recent posts as the user views the screen.

Smaller-scale applications can probably use simple notification systems for a while until they grow. But be aware that for every 10-fold increase in traffic or data, you may have to reconsider each architecture decision in your application. Monitor how well your current system is keeping up with traffic; test simulated traffic at least 10x the current traffic, and see if it still works.

Solution: Just Wake Me Up When We Get There

A good solution to replace the polling queries in Stas' code is a *task queue*. Like the solution in Chapter 10, Cacheless Transactions, on page 121, a task queue is one way to use a message queue—a separate technology that complements the database. Let's first understand the principle, then look at how you can implement it in the Visage application.

Understanding Task Queues

A task queue runs a code function of your choice in response to a message. In your application, you post to a broker service. Posting to the broker is quick, and your application is then free to run other code; for example, a web application can send a response to the user immediately, to let them know their request has been received. The broker triggers the backend to run the function to do the work asynchronously. This way, the user doesn't need to wait for the function to run before they get their response.

For the example in this chapter, we'll use Celery 5.5.3,[1] an open source task queue. Celery supports a variety of message queue or cache services as the broker. We'll use Valkey 9.0.0,[2] but you could also use Redis, RabbitMQ, Amazon SQS, or others. You can write the client and the back-end function in one of several supported programming languages. Python is a typical choice, and Visage is written in Python, so that's what we'll use.

The following diagram shows the application putting a value in the broker, then the broker triggers Celery to run the task, which also updates the database.

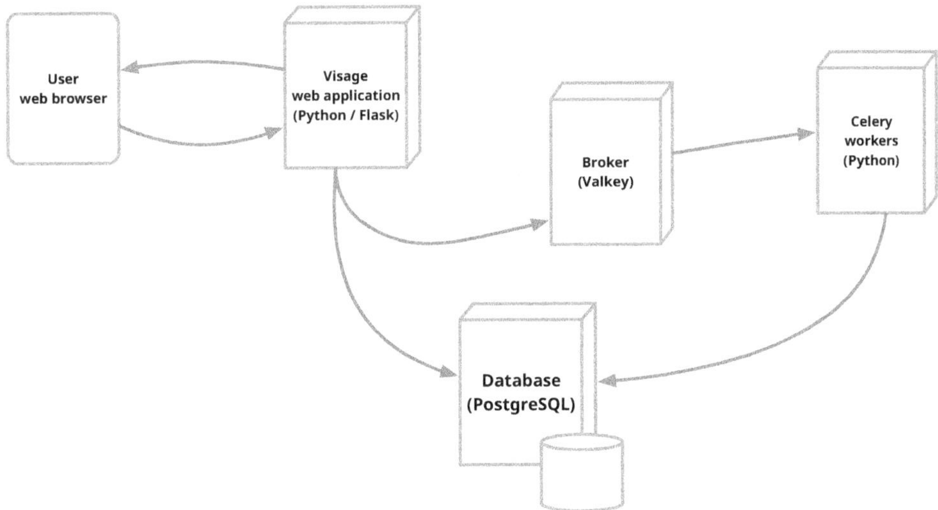

Redesigning Visage Notifications with Celery

Let's take a look at how we can integrate Celery into the application. Visage uses the Flask web application framework, so first we initialize Flask, and also initialize Celery, so Flask handlers can conveniently send messages to the Celery server. This code is general-purpose and would appear similar in any application that uses Flask and Celery:

Polling/soln/visage-celery.py

```
from celery import Celery, Task, shared_task
from flask import Flask, g, redirect, render_template, request
import psycopg2
from psycopg2.extras import RealDictCursor
import time
```

1. https://docs.celeryq.dev/
2. https://valkey.io/

The Three-Legged Stool

To build a scalable application architecture, you should have practical experience with the following three technologies so you know how to apply them:

- A *database* is the safe place to store the source of data.
- A *cache* is for high-speed, frequent access to a subset of the data.
- A *message queue* passes data between system components asynchronously. One use of a message queue is a task queue, as described in this chapter.

All three of these serve an important role. Like the legs of a three-legged stool, if you take one away, the platform won't be stable.

In a low-scale application, you can get by using the database as a cache or message queue, but as the scale of your application increases, you'll find that it has limits. To help grow your application to the next level, redesign your application to use a purpose-made cache or message queue product.

```
def celery_init_app(app: Flask) -> Celery:

    class FlaskTask(Task):
        def __call__(self, *args: object, **kwargs: object) -> object:
            with app.app_context():
                return self.run(*args, **kwargs)

    celery_app = Celery(app.name, task_cls=FlaskTask)
    celery_app.config_from_object(app.config["CELERY"])
    celery_app.set_default()
    app.extensions["celery"] = celery_app
    return celery_app

def create_app() -> Flask:
    app = Flask(__name__)
    app.config.from_mapping(
        CELERY=dict(
            broker_url="redis://localhost",
            result_backend="redis://localhost",
            task_ignore_result=True,
        ),
    )
    app.config.from_prefixed_env()
    celery_init_app(app)
    return app

flask_app = create_app()
celery_app = flask_app.extensions["celery"]
```

The next function is annotated as a handler for a Flask web route of the form submission handler when users write a new post. It inserts a row into the post table in the database. Then, after that's committed, it sends a message to the Celery task queue:

Polling/soln/visage-celery.py

```
@flask_app.route("/post_submit", methods=['POST'])
def post_submit():

    with psycopg2.connect("dbname='visage' host='localhost'") as conn:

        with conn.cursor() as cur:

            # Insert new post to database
            cur.execute("""
                INSERT INTO post (post_title, post_text, user_id)
                VALUES (%(post_title)s, %(post_text)s, %(user_id)s)
                RETURNING post_id
            """,
                        {'post_title': request.form['post_title'],
                         'post_text': request.form['post_text'],
                         'user_id': 1})
            new_post_id = cur.fetchone()[0]

    # Send message to a Celery task
    post_notify.delay(new_post_id)
    flask_app.logger.info(f"Enqueued new post_id: {new_post_id}")

    return redirect('/')
```

Lastly, the following code shows a function annotated as a Celery task (@shared_task()). This means post_notify isn't a normal function that runs in the same process as the Visage application when you call it. Instead, calling post_notify.delay() sends a message to the broker for the Celery server and returns. In this example, we also include an argument of the primary key of the new post row.

The code of the post_notify() function calls process_notifications(). We can pretend the latter function does the real work of notifying all users who have registered interest in the new post, but for demo purposes, that's simulated by a five-second sleep().

Once the notification work is done, the post_notify() function updates the post in the PostgreSQL database to record the fact that this work has been done:

Polling/soln/visage-celery.py

```
def process_notifications(post_id):
    flask_app.logger.info(f"Notify for post_id: {post_id}")
    time.sleep(5)

@shared_task()
def post_notify(post_id):

    process_notifications(post_id)

    with psycopg2.connect("dbname='visage' host='localhost'") as conn:
        with conn.cursor() as cur:
            cur.execute("""
```

```
        UPDATE post SET notified_at = NOW()
        WHERE post_id = %(post_id)s
    """, {'post_id': post_id})
```

Before the tasks can be processed, we have to start a separate process with the celery command. This process waits for events sent to the broker and invokes the respective task function:

Polling/soln/visage-celery.sh
```
celery -A visage-celery worker --loglevel=INFO
```

When we open the form and then submit it to write a new post, we can watch the log output of the Visage web application: it shows both web requests and the INFO output from the line we wrote in the post_submit() function.

```
127.0.0.1 - - [18/Nov/2025 19:40:12] "GET /post_form HTTP/1.1" 200 -
[2025-11-18 19:40:20,642] INFO in visage-celery: Enqueued new post_id: 2
127.0.0.1 - - [18/Nov/2025 19:40:20] "POST /post_submit HTTP/1.1" 302 -
```

The elapsed time of this request is less than 10 milliseconds.

While this is going on, we can also watch the log output of the Celery process. We see that it's woken up by the broker, and it knows it should invoke the post_notify task. It also shows how long it takes to do the simulated work of notifying users of the new post.

```
[2025-11-18 19:40:20,643: INFO/MainProcess] Task visage-celery.post_notify
  [c34c556b-b22c-4852-a8fe-523d0bac1e2d] received
[2025-11-18 19:40:20,647: INFO/ForkPoolWorker-8] Notify for post_id: 2
[2025-11-18 19:40:25,675: INFO/ForkPoolWorker-8] Task
  visage-celery.post_notify[c34c556b-b22c-4852-a8fe-523d0bac1e2d]
  succeeded in 5.028898290824145s: None
```

As expected, the task takes about five seconds.

You Have Arrived At Your Destination

The query traffic of a successful project tends to grow rapidly. In fact, that's probably your goal.

Dedicated message queue software products like RabbitMQ or ActiveMQ, or cloud services like Amazon SQS or Google Cloud PubSub, are designed to handle greater throughput than similar extensions operating as part of the RDBMS. They may also have more features, like high availability, message delivery options, and persistence.

Once you redesign the Visage notification system to use a task queue instead of polling queries, you're able to reduce the query load on the PostgreSQL server

> **Just Use PostgreSQL?**
>
> Could the RDBMS itself support a message queue feature to help applications implement a publish/subscribe pattern without the cost of frequent polling queries? PostgreSQL, for example, has a popular extension `pgmq` for this purpose and also special commands like `LISTEN` and `NOTIFY`. The book *Just Use Postgres!: A fast guide for developers [Mag25]* has a detailed chapter on using these features.
>
> It's true that these RDBMS extensions exist, and some software projects do use them. Avoiding the complexity of adding more software components to your project can be an advantage. You have fewer components to support, including administration, monitoring, and performing upgrades.
>
> If your project can be successful using simpler architecture, then go ahead and do that. But be aware that message queues implemented as an RDBMS extension have a scalability ceiling. You should monitor the throughput, and be prepared that someday, when you approach that limit, you will want to refactor to an architecture with more capacity.

so much that other queries are noticeably faster. You might even be able to deploy the database on a less expensive server and still support the lighter load.

Even Stas is so impressed with your progress that you finally get a reaction from him: "Hmph."

For every order of magnitude growth in traffic volume or data volume, take time to review your application architecture.

Mini-Antipattern: Enqueuing Before Committing

If you send a message to a queue before you commit data, it would look something like the following pseudocode:

```
START TRANSACTION;
 INSERT ROW;
 SEND MESSAGE TO QUEUE;
COMMIT;
```

The risk of this design is that the client at the other end of the queue might receive the message very quickly, in fact, before the database transaction commits. The client then acts on the message prematurely. It might try to read or update the row from the database, but since that client is running its own transaction, it's unable to query the row that hasn't been committed. Or it could send a notification, like an email, that references the new row.

The row might never get committed, for instance, if the application that inserted it crashes, or decides to roll back the transaction for some other reason. Then the client that receives the message will believe the row exists, but no one will ever see it.

These sorts of bugs are hard to track down because they may happen intermittently. It depends on how quickly the queue delivers that message.

When designing an application that uses a queue to message another part of your system, it's safer to commit first. The pseudocode would look like the following:

```
START TRANSACTION;
 INSERT ROW;
COMMIT;
SEND MESSAGE TO QUEUE;
```

This is a good way to reduce risk. The recipient can't receive the message before it is sent, and you make sure it is sent only after the data is safely committed in the database.

There is no logically necessary connection between events at different times; therefore nothing that is happening now or will happen in the future can disprove the hypothesis that the world began five minutes ago.

Bertrand Russell

CHAPTER 12

Transaction Encapsulation

"We have a new feature we want you to implement." The product manager, Terry, leans over the cubicle partition and holds up his hands, using his fingers to literally and figuratively frame the discussion. "The user view includes a link to that user's most recent post."

You blink and stare back at Terry. You'd just finished integrating Visage code with SQLAlchemy, an object-relational mapping (ORM) framework for Python. This refactors large portions of the code to *model* classes, which contain the data and logic for each domain, which typically correspond to database tables. You've wanted to improve the structure of the code in this way for a long time, but it was kind of mentally exhausting to make such a large change.

Your brain shifts to address Terry's sudden announcement of a new feature. "Uh ... so the user model needs a reference to their most recent post. Sounds like denormalization ... which means the user model has to be updated each time they write a new post? In a transaction?"

Terry waves a hand casually. "The implementation is up to you." He pivots into the break room to refill his coffee.

You open a code editor to inspect the newly refactored code of Visage to plan the best place to add the feature Terry said he wants. It doesn't sound like it's going to be too hard ...

Objective: Transactions for Multiple Models

One of the goals of your recent refactoring was to make the Flask routing functions shorter and simpler by moving code implementing database access into model classes. Models are a way of implementing a domain within the application. A domain is comprised of data elements and code to work with those data. In an object-oriented system, a class has data members and functions that use the respective data. This is an example of *encapsulation*. If the code that depends on a given table is in one class, then it's easier to update the code if the table ever changes.

The feature Terry wants affects two tables—`post` and `user`. By convention, each model implements data and actions for one table, so these tables are accessed by two models—classes `Post` and `User`, respectively. Your `Post` model already has a method `create()` which saves a row to the `post` table. You're sure you can write code to update the `user` table.

Since the code for each model is supposed to access only its respective table, it's not immediately clear how to ensure both models commit their changes atomically. It doesn't seem in the spirit of encapsulation if you update the `user` table in a method of the `Post` model.

This task seemed easy, but now there's an ambiguity about how the code should be organized.

Antipattern: Every Model Class Manages Its Transactions

It seems like a reasonable approach to delegate data changes to their respective models. The `Post` model needs to insert a row into the `post` table and then call a method of the `User` model to update the user.

The first step is to add a column to the `user` table:

Transaction/anti/alter-user.sql

```
ALTER TABLE "user"
  ADD COLUMN latest_post_id BIGINT REFERENCES post(post_id);
```

Now, at least there's a place to save the ID for the new post.

Attempt #1: Committing in Each Model

The code starts with initialization as shown in the following excerpt:

Transaction/anti/visage-transact-error.py

```
from datetime import datetime, timezone
from flask import Flask, redirect, render_template, request
from flask_sqlalchemy import SQLAlchemy
from sqlalchemy import ForeignKey, func
from sqlalchemy.orm import (DeclarativeBase, Mapped, mapped_column,
    relationship)
from typing import List

flask_app = Flask(__name__)
flask_app.config.from_mapping(
    SECRET_KEY="visage_key",
    SQLALCHEMY_DATABASE_URI="postgresql+psycopg2://localhost:5432/visage",
```

```
    SQLALCHEMY_ECHO=True,
)

class Base(DeclarativeBase):
  pass

db = SQLAlchemy(model_class=Base)
db.init_app(flask_app)
```

Note the Base class, which is derived from SQLAlchemy's DeclarativeBase. It's customary in an SQLAlchemy project to make a base class for all the models, so the preceding code is generic for any project.

The Post model starts with the following code:

Transaction/anti/visage-transact-error.py

```
class Post(db.Model):
    __tablename__ = "post"

    post_id: Mapped[int] = mapped_column(primary_key=True)
    post_title: Mapped[str]
    post_text: Mapped[str]
    created_at: Mapped[datetime] = mapped_column(
            default=lambda: datetime.now(timezone.utc))
    updated_at: Mapped[datetime] = mapped_column(
            default=lambda: datetime.now(timezone.utc),
            onupdate=lambda: datetime.now(timezone.utc))
    user_id: Mapped[int] = mapped_column(ForeignKey("user.user_id"))
    user: Mapped["User"] = relationship("User", back_populates="posts")

    @staticmethod
    def get_recent(n):
        with db.session.begin():
            recent_posts = db.session.execute(
                db.select(
                    Post.post_title,
                    func.left(Post.post_text, 100).label("post_text_short"),
                    User.display_name).
                select_from(Post).
                join(Post.user).
                order_by(Post.updated_at.desc()).
                limit(4)
            )
        return recent_posts

    @staticmethod
    def create(user_id, title, text):
        with db.session.begin():
            post = Post(post_title=title, post_text=text, user_id=user_id)
            db.session.add(post)
            db.session.flush()

            User.set_latest(user_id, post.post_id)
```

The preceding model code uses SQLAlchemy's declarative style to define properties corresponding to table columns.

The model's method get_recent() runs the query to get the most recent few posts for the home page. This is used by the application's home page.

The create() method is called when a user submits the form to create a new post.

The last line of the create() method has the new feature you need; it calls a method in the User model to update the user and save the reference to the new post.

The User model declares its own properties. Then, you need to implement the set_latest() method, which updates the new column of the user table:

Transaction/anti/visage-transact-error.py

```
class User(db.Model):
    __tablename__ = "user"

    user_id: Mapped[int] = mapped_column(primary_key=True)
    user_type_id: Mapped[int]
    display_name: Mapped[str]
    real_name: Mapped[str]
    latest_post_id: Mapped[int]
    posts: Mapped[List["Post"]] = relationship(back_populates="user")

    @staticmethod
    def set_latest(user_id, post_id):
        with db.session.begin():
            db.session.execute(
                db.update(User).
                where(User.user_id == user_id).
                values(latest_post_id = post_id)
            )
```

This implementation looks good so far. It honors your design to delegate work to each respective model and keep the code for the routes short and tidy, which you can see in the following final excerpt:

Transaction/anti/visage-transact-error.py

```
@flask_app.route("/")
def home():
    recent_posts = Post.get_recent(4)
    return render_template("home.html",
                           recent_posts=recent_posts)

@flask_app.route("/post_form", methods=['GET'])
def post():
    return render_template("post_form.html")

@flask_app.route("/post_submit", methods=['POST'])
```

```
def post_submit():
    Post.create(1, request.form["post_title"], request.form["post_text"])
    return redirect('/')

if __name__ == "__main__":
    flask_app.run(port=8080, debug=True)
```

But as soon as you try to test this code, you see an error output to the application log like the following example:

```
2025-11-24 16:14:11,073 INFO sqlalchemy.engine.Engine ROLLBACK
[2025-11-24 16:14:11,074] ERROR in app: Exception on /post_submit [POST]
  File "visage-transact.error.py", line 74, in set_latest
    with db.session.begin():
         ~~~~~~~~~~~~~~~~^^
sqlalchemy.exc.InvalidRequestError: A transaction is already begun
  on this Session.
127.0.0.1 - - [24/Nov/2025 16:14:11] "POST /post_submit HTTP/1.1" 500 -
```

Each model method had to start and commit its own transaction because it couldn't assume its caller had done so.

But if the caller *has* started a transaction, this is a problem. In many SQL implementations, starting a redundant transaction while the session already has a transaction in progress doesn't work. A session can have only one active transaction.

In the sequence diagram at the top of the next page, you can see the order of operations. If the Post model begins a transaction and then calls a method of the User model while the transaction is still active, it results in an error.

Clearly, you need another approach.

Attempt #2: Using a Transaction Flag

You need to avoid starting and committing transactions in models that are called by other models. In this case, User.set_latest() should apply its update but not start its own transaction. It should just piggyback on the transaction of its caller, Post.create(). But User.set_latest() might be called by some other caller, so it still needs code to start a transaction—sometimes.

The following example shows how you could code this using an optional *flag argument* to the method. For example, call the flag do_transaction. If it's True (the default), then User.set_latest() should start and commit its own transaction. If it's False, then skip the transaction.

Post.create() calls User.set_latest(), setting the flag to False as shown in the following implementation:

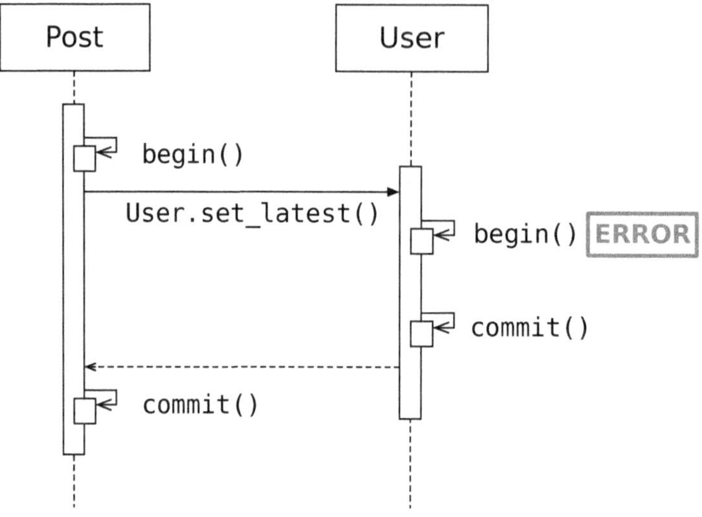

Transaction/anti/visage-transact-flag.py

```
@staticmethod
def create(user_id, title, text):
    with db.session.begin():
        post = Post(post_title=title, post_text=text, user_id=user_id)
        db.session.add(post)
        db.session.flush()

        User.set_latest(user_id, post.post_id, do_transaction=False)
```

User.set_latest() accepts the flag and runs the update either in a transaction or not, shown in the following method:

Transaction/anti/visage-transact-flag.py

```
@staticmethod
def set_latest(user_id, post_id, do_transaction=True):
    if do_transaction:
        with db.session.begin():
            db.session.execute(
                db.update(User).
                where(User.user_id == user_id).
                values(latest_post_id = post_id)
            )
    else:
        db.session.execute(
            db.update(User).
            where(User.user_id == user_id).
            values(latest_post_id = post_id)
        )
```

This duplicates the code for the action of this method, once in a transaction context block, and once without that context, so it relies on the caller's transaction. This conflicts with the well-known programming principle of DRY (Don't Repeat Yourself), which discourages such duplication of code.

It's also an example of *Control Coupling*, or passing a flag to a method that instructs that method which code path to run.

Modules should be free to change their implementation independently of callers. But if some kind of coupling exists between modules, a code change can cause ripple effects in another module. That tends to increase the cost and risk of making changes, so the general wisdom is that we should reduce coupling where possible.[1]

Even though the coupling between the Post and User models seems like it might work, it feels wrong. You decide it's better to avoid it, and you look for other solutions.

Attempt #3: Implementing Dummy Transactions

Is there a way the code could request a transaction start or commit, but make those operations no-ops if it can detect that there's already an active transaction in progress? Surely, this is something the framework can be adapted to do.

You can change the Base model class to track active transaction state. Add a new class variable transaction_nest_level. If that level is zero, starting a transaction really does start a transaction and also increments the variable. Subsequent requests, therefore, know that a transaction is already active, and they don't try to start another one. The variable is incremented even if the start transaction is a no-op, so it counts how many nested levels were requested, and knows how many of these fake transactions must be resolved eventually.

Likewise, commit (or rollback) is a no-op if the variable is greater than zero. Each request to resolve a transaction decrements the variable, and once it reaches zero, then it's time to really commit or rollback.

You can add these methods to the Base class as follows:

Transaction/anti/visage-transact-nested.py
```
class Base(DeclarativeBase):
    transaction_nest_level = 0

    def begin_transaction(s):
        if Base.transaction_nest_level == 0:
            s.begin()
```

1. https://wiki.c2.com/?CouplingAndCohesion

```
            flask_app.logger.debug("REAL begin transaction")
        else:
            flask_app.logger.debug("NO-OP begin transaction")
        Base.transaction_nest_level += 1

    def commit_transaction(s):
        Base.transaction_nest_level -= 1
        if Base.transaction_nest_level == 0:
            flask_app.logger.debug("REAL commit transaction")
            s.commit()
        else:
            flask_app.logger.debug("NO-OP commit transaction")

    def rollback_transaction(s):
        Base.transaction_nest_level -= 1
        if Base.transaction_nest_level == 0:
            flask_app.logger.debug("REAL rollback transaction")
            s.rollback()
        else:
            flask_app.logger.debug("NO-OP rollback transaction")
```

Using conditional transactions in model methods is pretty straightforward. It's not quite as elegant as using a Python context manager (the with statement), but it's clear enough. The following change to the Post.create() method wraps the insert in exception handling, so the transaction will request a rollback if any errors occur:

Transaction/anti/visage-transact-nested.py

```
@staticmethod
def create(user_id, title, text):
    Base.begin_transaction(db.session)
    try:
        post = Post(post_title=title, post_text=text, user_id=user_id)
        db.session.add(post)
        db.session.flush()
        User.set_latest(user_id, post.post_id)
    except:
        Base.rollback_transaction(db.session)
    finally:
        Base.commit_transaction(db.session)
```

The User.set_latest() method is changed in a similar way, as shown in the following excerpt:

Transaction/anti/visage-transact-nested.py

```
@staticmethod
def set_latest(user_id, post_id):
    Base.begin_transaction(db.session)
    try:
        db.session.execute(
            db.update(User).
```

```
            where(User.user_id == user_id).
            values(latest_post_id = post_id)
        )
    except:
        Base.rollback_transaction(db.session)
    finally:
        Base.commit_transaction(db.session)
```

Now, the code for both methods should automatically make a transaction, or skip making a transaction, depending on whether it's called from the top level or from a nested level.

Is this finally a working solution? Let's consider some of the ways it can fail.

Pitfalls of Dummy Rollbacks and Commits

The solution works only if every change succeeds and commits. If one of the transactions rolls back, strange things happen.

If the nested transaction in the User model rolls back because of an error, but the outer transaction in the Post model commits, then both changes will commit, even though the User model requested to roll back its change.

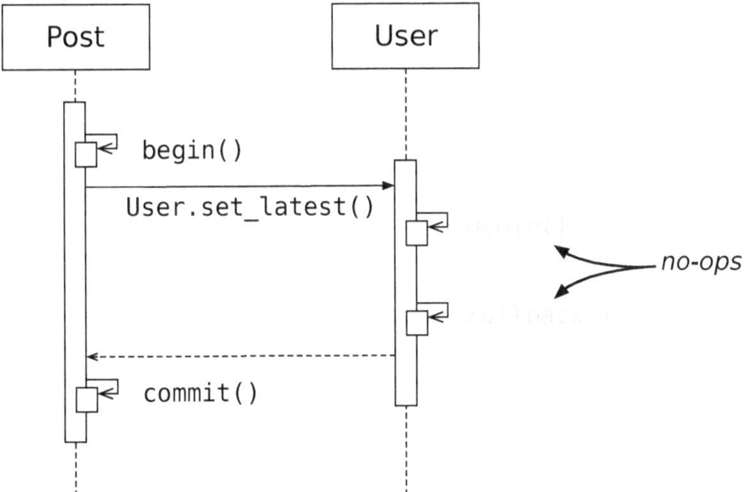

The reverse can also happen. If the nested transaction commits, but the outer transaction rolls back, then both changes will roll back, even though the User model requested to commit. This is shown in the diagram at the top of the next page.

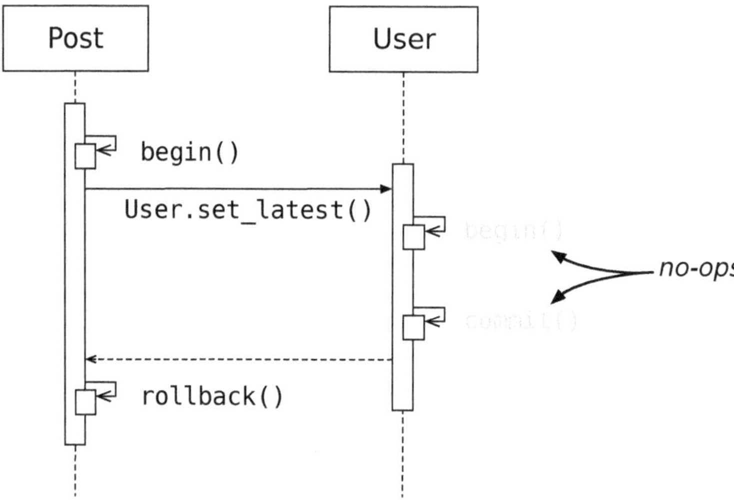

This is a problem with implementing no-op transactions. Models request a commit or a rollback, but they have no way of ensuring their request takes effect. Interfaces that pretend to honor the caller's request, but silently ignore it, make applications unpredictable and hard to debug.

Which Database Frameworks Implemented Dummy Transactions?

The pattern of making transaction commands no-ops or dummy commands has been implemented in several popular database interfaces for multiple programming languages. Most of these projects eventually deprecated the feature once they learned that it caused more trouble than it was worth. The following list includes some examples, although it's not a comprehensive survey:

- SQLAlchemy for Python: Deprecated no-op transactions in version 1.4, and removed them in 2.0. Nested transactions may be implemented with transaction savepoints.
- Doctrine Database Abstraction Layer for PHP: Deprecated no-op transactions in version 3.4, and removed them in 4.0. Nested transactions may be implemented with transaction savepoints.
- Propel for PHP: Continues to support no-op transactions as of version 2.0.

Nonstandard SQL Products

In standard SQL, trying to start a transaction while another transaction is already active is an error. Some SQL products have different behavior from this standard.

For example, Microsoft SQL Server and Sybase allow so-called *nested transactions*—starting a new transaction while another transaction is active isn't an error. The way these nested transactions work may confuse or surprise developers. You can begin several nested levels of transactions, but you must resolve all of these levels to finally commit. If you roll back at *any* level, then *all* of the changes are discarded.

How to Recognize the Antipattern

- "How can I detect that a transaction has already been started?"

  This is a sign that the developer is thinking of implementing the antipattern, making some transactions no-ops.

- "The log shows that a change was committed, but when I check the data, I don't see the result that should be there."

  Mysterious data anomalies may occur because some transaction requests are ignored. Commits and rollbacks don't behave as expected. Even transaction isolation may cause confusion because a snapshot began earlier than you think, based on the code.

- "Where does transaction management belong in a model class?"

  This is a trick question because after several tries to make it work, we're starting to understand that transaction management might not belong in a model class at all.

Legitimate Uses of the Antipattern

The antipattern in this chapter is a rare case that has no legitimate exception case. Software developers underestimate how important it is for transactions to start and end predictably. You should use coding habits that make transactions work as you intend.

Solution: Simplify, Simplify

The solution to this problem is surprisingly simple: not all code that calls database methods must be placed in a model class.

What Is a Model?

The Model-View-Controller (MVC) pattern dates back to a 1979 research project at Xerox PARC.[a]

The original description of MVC in that project did not say that a model had to be a 1-for-1 representation of one database table:

> *The models are represented in the computer as a collection of data together with the methods necessary to process these data.*

Likewise, each table may be represented by multiple models.

Over the years, it became a convention to make a model coincident for each table. To preserve the abstraction, it became popular to assume that all database-related actions are implemented within the model interface. Today, many developers don't question this. They practically use "model" and "table" interchangeably.

We should keep in mind that this is only a convention. It's possible that this convention doesn't serve us well when it comes to transaction actions.

a. https://folk.universitetetioslo.no/trygver/themes/mvc/mvc-index.html

If you were choosing where to define variables for some other kind of application data, you wouldn't define them as class variables if multiple classes needed to access them. You'd define the variables outside of any of those classes, and let the classes reference them either as parameters by reference or as global data.

The same is true of transactions. A transaction is a resource shared among model classes in the same way that the database session is shared.

Let's take a look at how easy it is to implement the Visage application once you treat a transaction as part of the database session.

Using Transactions at Session Scope

The only code you need to begin and commit the transaction is in the route method that calls the models. In an MVC application, this is part of the *controller*, not the models.

You can write this code with explicit `try` and `except` blocks, calling `commit()` as the last action of the try block, and `rollback()` in case an error occurred.

With this pattern, all the database changes made by the models called in this route either succeed or fail as a group.

Transaction/soln/visage-transact.py
```
@flask_app.route("/post_submit", methods=['POST'])
def post_submit():
    with db.session.begin():
        Post.create(1, request.form["post_title"], request.form["post_text"])
    return redirect('/')
```

An alternative way of writing this code is to use try and except blocks. You'd do this if you needed to add code to log the error or retry the action, or any other case where you needed to do something special along with the commit or rollback.

Transaction/soln/visage-transact-try.py
```
@flask_app.route("/post_submit", methods=['POST'])
def post_submit():
    db.session.begin()
    try:
        Post.create(1, request.form["post_title"], request.form["post_text"])
        db.session.commit()
    except:
        db.session.rollback()
        raise
    return redirect('/')
```

Neither of the models needs to begin or commit their own transactions in this solution. Models rely on their caller to manage the transaction, and they assume that the caller will decide if the whole unit of work will be committed or rolled back.

The following implementation of Post.create() is simpler because it needs no transaction-management calls:

Transaction/soln/visage-transact.py
```
@staticmethod
def create(user_id, title, text):
    post = Post(post_title=title, post_text=text, user_id=user_id)
    db.session.add(post)
    db.session.flush()

    User.set_latest(user_id, post.post_id)
```

The same is true for the following implementation of User.set_latest():

Transaction/soln/visage-transact.py
```
@staticmethod
def set_latest(user_id, post_id):
    db.session.execute(
        update(User).
        where(User.user_id == user_id).
        values(latest_post_id = post_id)
    )
```

Managing the transaction outside the models is much easier than any of the attempts to manage transactions within model methods. By now, you should feel more confident about delivering the feature Terry wanted on schedule, without compromising your refactoring of the application code into model classes.

Transactions operate at the session level, not at the model level.

Mini-Antipattern: ORMs That Pluralize Table Names

In the previous example, the names of the model classes and their respective tables are similar, except for the capitalization. In SQLAlchemy, to make it clear which table name to use, we declare it with the attribute `__tablename__`.

```
class Post(db.Model):
    __tablename__ = "post"
```

Some ORM frameworks use a convention that model classes are named as a singular noun (`Post` or `User`), while the table for that model is the plural form of that noun (`posts` or `users`). By using this convention, they reason, the ORM code can generate SQL for common queries, substituting the plural form of the class name in SQL.

But they didn't account for the complex rules for plurals in English.

The Ruby on Rails `ActiveSupport::Inflector` class includes a `pluralize` method that transforms nouns to their plural form. Testing words that cover most English pluralization rules,[2] this method fails to return the correct plural for 73 out of 208 of the words. The failures include some words that might be meaningful model names in a database for business, education, science, or games, such as *appendix, cargo, curriculum, genus, hero,* or *status.*

The Rails project decided not to fix cases of incorrect pluralization[3] to avoid breaking backward compatibility for existing projects that rely on the current Rails inflection code. Instead, you have to know which words the Rails inflector handles incorrectly, and then fix them yourself using custom configuration.

Besides Rails, some other ORM packages try to convert singular model names to plural table names by default. For example, GORM for Go, Sequelize for

2. https://en.wikipedia.org/wiki/English_plurals
3. https://api.rubyonrails.org/classes/ActiveSupport/Inflector.html

Node.js, and EF Core for .NET. Each of these has its own implementation of pluralization rules, and they all fail on slightly different sets of words.

Is pluralizing table names a good use of your time as a programmer, given that this feature has no value to users of your software product?

Other ORM packages use a better strategy: the names of a model and its table are spelled exactly the same by default, unless the developer declares the table name explicitly.

Delay always breeds danger; and to protract a great design is often to ruin it.

Miguel de Cervantes

CHAPTER 13

Fear of Deadlocks

Terry, the product manager, is back in your office. "Hey, there's a top priority bug about to hit your inbox. Support is getting hammered."

You're guessing that what Terry means by "hammered" is that the bug was reported by more than one customer.

"Visage is intermittently throwing a big ugly error message about a deadlock," Terry explains. "That's bad user experience. I want you to make sure no deadlocks happen. *None.*" He makes a circle with his fingers and silently mouths the word, "zero."

Then he's gone again.

When you see the bug report, it says the error happens—sometimes—when editing users to set a friend. This is a feature that was recently added to allow Visage users to select one designated friend as a backup contact. It works almost every time, so the feature was released and is now used publicly. But apparently, in rare cases, it fails for mysterious reasons.

This is going to make it hard to troubleshoot.

Objective: Don't See Deadlock Errors

The best place to start looking is the code for the new feature.

The Visage web route handler for setting a friend is in the following short function:

Deadlocks/anti/visage-deadlock.py

```
@flask_app.route("/set_friend", methods=['POST'])
def set_friend_submit():
    User.set_friend(request.form["user_id"], request.form["friend_user_id"])
    return redirect('/users')
```

That simply calls the User model's set_friend() method, which looks like the following (omitting the model's attribute declarations, shown in detail in Chapter 12, Transaction Encapsulation, on page 149):

Deadlocks/anti/visage-deadlock.py
```
class User(db.Model):
    __tablename__ = "user"

    # ...

    @staticmethod
    def set_friend(user_id, friend_user_id):
        with db.session.begin():
            db.session.execute(
                db.update(User).
                where(User.user_id == user_id).
                values(friend_user_id = friend_user_id)
            )

            db.session.execute(
                db.update(User).
                where(User.user_id == friend_user_id).
                values(friend_user_id = user_id)
            )
```

Setting a user's friend runs updates in a transaction to set the friend on two rows. The effect is that the two users in a new friend relationship reference each other. Somehow, this causes the deadlock error.

The next step of troubleshooting is to try to reproduce the error. The bug report you read says the deadlock occurs intermittently, but it also says that *both* users who requested the change were annoyed by the error. This clue makes you think that when the two users simultaneously submit the request, their SQL queries are conflicting somehow.

You insert a five-second delay between the two updates, as shown in the following modified code:

Deadlocks/anti/visage-deadlock-sleep.py
```
@staticmethod
def set_friend(user_id, friend_user_id):
    with db.session.begin():
        db.session.execute(
            db.update(User).
            where(User.user_id == user_id).
            values(friend_user_id = friend_user_id)
        )

        # Test the deadlock by adding a sleep between the two updates.
        flask_app.logger.debug("sleeping 5 seconds")
        sleep(5)
```

```
        db.session.execute(
            db.update(User).
            where(User.user_id == friend_user_id).
            values(friend_user_id = user_id)
        )
```

Then, you run this modified instance of the Visage application on your development environment, and open two browser windows to the user's screen. You're trying to simulate two users submitting the form simultaneously, each requesting their side of the friend request.

In this test, Bud requests to be Lou's friend, and at the same time, Lou requests to be Bud's friend. You prepare each browser window to look like the following, and then click the Submit buttons of both windows. If you click them within five seconds, then the two requests will be interleaved, so they both run their first update, then start a five-second sleep before the second update.

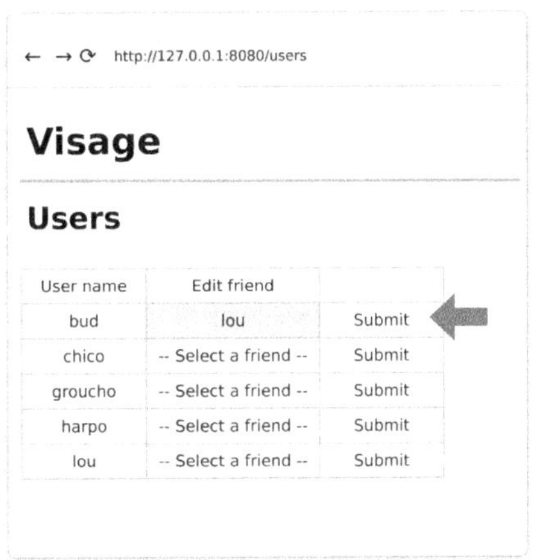

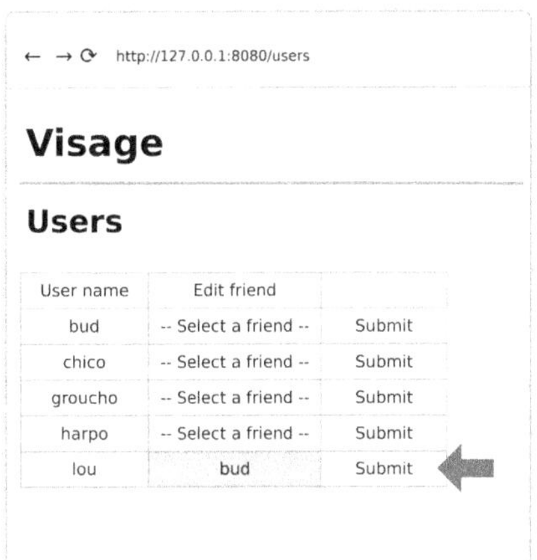

Bingo! You see the following deadlock error in one browser window:

```
sqlalchemy.exc.OperationalError: (psycopg2.errors.DeadlockDetected)
DETAIL:  Process 31370 waits for ShareLock on transaction 1957;
  blocked by process 31366.
Process 31366 waits for ShareLock on transaction 1958;
  blocked by process 31370.
HINT:  See server log for query details.
CONTEXT:  while updating tuple (0,22) in relation "user"

[SQL: UPDATE "user" SET friend_user_id=%(friend_user_id)s
  WHERE "user".user_id = %(user_id_1)s]
[parameters: {'friend_user_id': '2', 'user_id_1': '1'}]
(Background on this error at: https://sqlalche.me/e/20/e3q8)
```

The error names two processes, 31366 and 31370. Each has tried to run its second update, but encountered a lock conflict because the other process already had that row locked. A database like PostgreSQL detects this and immediately terminates one or the other session. When two processes are stuck waiting for each other, then neither will give up the lock they already have. That's what a deadlock is. No amount of waiting will resolve this state, so the best thing for the database to do is interrupt it.

Now that you can reproduce the error, it's time to try to address the product manager's request.

Antipattern: Trying to Prevent All Deadlocks

You and your team brainstorm several possible solutions to prevent deadlocks. One by one, you can try them.

Let's look at the ideas the team comes up with.

Make Transactions Quicker

The deadlock happens when the two processes run their updates in an interleaved manner. Anthony says that it stands to reason that making the moment between the updates more brief will reduce the chance of the deadlock. In this case, there's not much opportunity to make the code faster, since there are no lines of code between the updates. Maybe a more powerful database server would run the code faster.

Gordon Letwin, a software architect at Microsoft in its early years, reportedly said:

```
In our business, one in a million is next Tuesday.
```

What he meant was that an event that has a very small chance of happening will happen sooner than you think, given the rate at which software tends to repeat the conditions for that event.

In other words, you can reduce the chance of deadlock, but that won't *prevent* one. It may occur less frequently, but it will still occur sometimes.

Limit Transactions to One Lock Request

Cleo's idea is that the problem occurs when two updates are run within a single transaction, so we should start and commit a transaction for each individual update. See the following change to the `set_friend()` method:

Deadlocks vs. Lock-Waits

Some software developers have the habit of using the term *deadlock* to describe a simpler case of one process waiting for a lock held by the second process. The second process isn't blocked; it's free to finish its work and then release the lock it's holding. Then the first process that was waiting can acquire the lock and do its own work. No deadlock occurs, and neither process needs to be interrupted by the database.

This case is properly called a *lock-wait*. This is common in a system that has concurrent requests. Lock-waits usually resolve quickly without error, assuming your code is designed to finish transactions promptly.

Deadlocks/anti/visage-deadlock-transactions.py

```
@staticmethod
def set_friend(user_id, friend_user_id):
    with db.session.begin():
        db.session.execute(
            db.update(User).
            where(User.user_id == user_id).
            values(friend_user_id = friend_user_id)
        )

    with db.session.begin():
        db.session.execute(
            db.update(User).
            where(User.user_id == friend_user_id).
            values(friend_user_id = user_id)
        )
```

Once the first transaction commits, it releases any locks, allowing a second process to proceed. This means two processes won't deadlock even if they execute updates in an interleaved manner.

However, it's important that a transaction ensures changes are committed together. If each update commits individually, there's a chance the first update succeeds but the second update fails. This could occur if the Visage application is interrupted, or the database software crashes, or the database server crashes.

These conditions might be very unlikely, but they're not impossible.

Use Pessimistic Locking

Interleaved updates lead to a deadlock because the updates use *optimistic locking*. This term means that locks are not acquired until each update requests them. It's called optimistic because each process trusts that its second update won't have any problem acquiring the locks it needs.

Rafael's alternative is to use *pessimistic locking*, or forcing the process to get all locks it needs in one action, before attempting either update. By making the lock request atomic, it either succeeds for all locks or it doesn't.

One way to do this is to update both rows in one SQL statement. This works, but the update syntax to affect multiple rows is more complex. Some developers find it more time-consuming to puzzle through code like this. The following example shows the update conditionally sets different values on two rows:

Deadlocks/anti/visage-deadlock-atomic.py

```
@staticmethod
def set_friend(user_id, friend_user_id):
    with db.session.begin():
        db.session.execute(
            db.update(User).
            where(
                (User.user_id == user_id) |
                (User.user_id == friend_user_id)
            ).
            values(friend_user_id = case(
                (User.user_id == user_id, int(friend_user_id)),
                (User.user_id == friend_user_id, int(user_id))
            ))
        )
```

A second way to do this is to use a table lock or an advisory lock. This also works, but by locking the whole table, it blocks all processes, so they have to access the table serially. Even other processes doing unrelated updates against the same table will have to wait. The following shows the use of a table lock:

Deadlocks/anti/visage-deadlock-lock-table.py

```
@staticmethod
def set_friend(user_id, friend_user_id):
    with db.session.begin():
        db.session.execute(text("""
            LOCK TABLE "user" IN EXCLUSIVE MODE
        """))

        db.session.execute(
            db.update(User).
            where(User.user_id == user_id).
            values(friend_user_id = friend_user_id)
        )

        db.session.execute(
            db.update(User).
            where(User.user_id == friend_user_id).
            values(friend_user_id = user_id)
        )
```

Pessimistic locks tend to be too coarse-grained; they lock much more than the rows that need to be updated.

Ensure a Consistent Order for Locking

The intern Hayden says the solution (according to his computer science textbook) is to make sure the locks are requested in the same order in both processes.

The problem that caused the deadlock is that each process first acquires locks on different rows (the rows for two different users), then they both try to get locks on the rows each other has locked. If they were to request the *same* row first, then the deadlock couldn't happen. One would get the lock first, then the other would have to wait until the first process finished its transaction and released the locks on both rows.

The following code implements this by sorting the arguments with Python's sorted() function. Even when one process calls the method with arguments (1, 2) and the other process calls it with arguments (2, 1), both will sort the arguments into an array [1, 2]. Therefore, both processes will try to update the row for user_id = 1 first.

Deadlocks/anti/visage-deadlock-ordering.py

```
@staticmethod
def set_friend(user_id, friend_user_id):

    id = sorted([user_id, friend_user_id])

    with db.session.begin():
        db.session.execute(
            db.update(User).
            where(User.user_id == id[0]).
            values(friend_user_id = id[1])
        )

        db.session.execute(
            db.update(User).
            where(User.user_id == id[1]).
            values(friend_user_id = id[0])
        )
```

This solution isn't possible if the code needs to lock one row before it knows which row to lock for the second update.

It's also not possible if the rows can't be ordered—for example, suppose the rows to update have the same value.

Use a Task Queue

Stas speaks up. His idea is to use the task queue (he's become a fan of task queues since you showed him how to use Celery in Chapter 11, Polling: Are We There Yet?, on page 137).

Deadlocks occur when two or more processes try to run transactions concurrently and block each other's updates to the same set of rows. Stas explains that if both processes add their requests to a task queue, then a worker process will get notified and execute the updates serially. That way, they can't deadlock.

The team is uncertain. A task queue adds complexity and potential failures to the code on every request, even when it's unnecessary because it's unusual for requests to occur simultaneously. Also, this would require more code to synchronize the result to the client because the user screen needs to show the result of the update immediately.

The team decides they need a solution that has a simpler path during the majority of requests, and treats conflicts as exception cases.

Pros and Cons

Some of the preceding solutions are partially helpful, but they aren't effective in all cases, or they require unwanted compromises. You and your team may be stumped, but read on to see other solutions.

How to Recognize the Antipattern

- "We need to prevent all deadlocks."

  This is hard to guarantee, unless you sacrifice concurrency in a way that will probably hurt the scalability of your application. Preventing all deadlocks is not a good goal in most cases.

- "What are the chances of this edge case happening?"

  You might think that the case is rare if it depends on the collision of two arbitrary events, but as the number of concurrent events grows, it quickly becomes more likely. If you shoot an arrow into the sky, the chance that another arrow hits it is low. But if you shoot a hundred arrows at the same time, the chance that some pair of them will contact each other is surprisingly high. This is known as the Birthday Paradox.[1]

---

1. https://betterexplained.com/articles/understanding-the-birthday-paradox/

Legitimate Uses of the Antipattern

The separation of antipattern and solution in this chapter is more nuanced than in other chapters because many of the approaches in the antipattern section are actually helpful and can be used in some circumstances. It's worthwhile to try to reduce the chance of deadlocks by coding defensively, and architectural solutions like task queues have their place.

But none of the preceding approaches is a full solution that prevents deadlocks in all cases. That leads to the question: have we been trying to solve the wrong problem all along? The next section addresses this.

Solution: Mitigate Deadlocks

Suddenly, as though everyone on your team thought of it simultaneously, you all had the bright idea: instead of trying so hard to *prevent* deadlocks, what if you *handle* deadlocks when they occur? After all, they don't occur often, only in exceptional cases. So, most of the time, the updates execute with no problem.

Retry Transactions After Deadlock Exceptions

Together, you and your team develop the following implementation that detects deadlocks and automatically retries the transaction:

Deadlocks/soln/visage-deadlock-retry.py

```
from sqlalchemy.exc import OperationalError
from psycopg2.errors import DeadlockDetected

# ...

    @staticmethod
    def set_friend(user_id, friend_user_id, retries=3):

        wait_time = 1
        while retries > 0:
            try:
                with db.session.begin():
                    db.session.execute(
                        db.update(User).
                        where(User.user_id == user_id).
                        values(friend_user_id = friend_user_id)
                    )

                    db.session.execute(
                        db.update(User).
                        where(User.user_id == friend_user_id).
                        values(friend_user_id = user_id)
                    )
```

```
            return

        except OperationalError as err:
            if isinstance(err.orig, DeadlockDetected):
                flask_app.logger.warning("Deadlock detected, retrying")
                sleep(wait_time)
                retries -= 1
                wait_time *= 2
            else:
                raise err

    raise Exception("Maximum deadlock retries exceeded")
```

Inside the try block, this code looks like the original transaction block for two updates for rows in the user table. If the transaction succeeds, then it commits, and the code simply returns.

But if a deadlock occurs, the whole block is inside a loop to retry a few times. Each retry starts a new transaction, releasing its previous locks, and allowing the other process to finish. The new transaction acquires new locks, with a lesser risk of deadlock because the other process has also released its locks when it finished.

While this technically doesn't prevent deadlocks, the chances of the *same* deadlock happening multiple times in a short span of time are very unlikely. This is further mitigated by a short sleep, which gets longer on each retry. If it retries too many times and still can't succeed, it raises a final exception.

This is the best you can do. The product manager and the customer support team will have to be satisfied with this mitigation.

Deadlocks are a natural part of concurrent systems. You don't need to prevent deadlocks, but you do need to account for them.

Mini-Antipattern: Sharing Connections Between Threads

If your application is multithreaded, can you use the same database connection from multiple threads at the same time?

In general, the answer is no because a client/server SQL protocol is by nature a *stateful protocol*. In a stateful protocol, a message sent to the database or received from the database depends on the cumulative state created by previous actions.

For example, if you start a transaction, then subsequent queries on that connection are implicitly part of the transaction until you commit.

Likewise, when you execute a query, fetching from that connection returns results for that query.

If you share a connection between asynchronous threads in your application, each thread changes the state of the connection, for instance, by starting or committing a transaction, or executing a new query. The other threads using that connection don't coordinate with those actions. Since multiple threads using the same connection each assume that they're the only client using it, they'll get confused about the responses.

You should ensure that a connection is used exclusively by one thread until its actions and responses have been resolved, then hand off that connection so another thread can use it.

By analogy, this is like checking a book out of a library, reading it until you're finished, and returning it so another person can check it out.

In fact, this is basically how *connection pools* work. A client thread requests a connection from a connection pool, uses it for a transaction, and releases it back to the pool. When another thread requests its own connection, it may be the same one recently returned to the pool.

The point is to manage access to each connection, so independently executing threads in an application don't mix up their messages.

Fill your bowl to the brim, and it will spill.

Lao Tzu

CHAPTER 14

Data Hoarding and Sharding

BREEEP! The familiar pager alert sound goes off.

Most of the time, these alerts are spurious, triggered by brief spikes in Visage query traffic or transient web API failures. No need for you to take action. But you have to check the cause of the alert just in case it's something serious. This time, the alert message includes the following:

```
Disk space running low: 94372 of 4718592 MiB remaining.
```

This is alarming—the server was recently upgraded to a 4.5 TiB storage volume, and now it's 98 percent full! It should be less than 50 percent. You need to drop what you're doing and find out what's using up so much space.

You find a table in the Visage database that you don't recognize:

Sharding/log.sql

```
CREATE TABLE log (
  log_id BIGSERIAL PRIMARY KEY,
  log_type INT,
  log_data JSONB,
  created_at TIMESTAMP NOT NULL DEFAULT CURRENT_TIMESTAMP
);
```

It's called simply `log`, and it is already so large that this table accounts for most of the unexpected filling of your storage.

Investigating the Visage code, you identify some new SQL code written by Aaron, a new developer who recently joined the team. The new code inserts a large JSON document to the `log` table after every kind of action performed by the Visage application—every post edited, every comment written, every user login and logout, every notification sent, and every page view. The JSON document includes details about every web request, and there are over 100 million rows in the `log` table so far.

You head over to Aaron's desk. "Aaron, can I ask what this log table is for?" you ask, trying to keep calm. "Why do we need to store that much data?"

Aaron looks up. "I used to work in customer support," he explains. "Sometimes we'd get a call asking us to troubleshoot something for a customer, and having more data would have helped us."

"These customer issues need this much information?" you ask.

Aaron shrugs. "Customers might ask about anything, and we don't know what troubleshooting information we'll need until their call comes in. So, I figured saving everything I could think of would give us the best chance of having the right data when we need it. He sees the expression on your face and adds, "Siobhán approved this code."

You have another question. "How long do you need to keep this information? Can you expire the data after a day or so?"

Aaron smiles. "Yeah, I was thinking about that, too. But I wasn't sure if one day was long enough. I emailed the support team to give me an estimate for how long they would need troubleshooting data to be kept, but they haven't gotten back to me yet."

"So, you implemented no expiration," you say flatly. "But you still decided to write the code to save all that data, and then deployed to production."

"Yeah, I guess so," Aaron replies casually. "Is that a problem?"

Objective: Cope with Data Bloat

Obviously, the log table is growing too fast. Very soon, it will consume all the space on the database server, and then there won't be any space for the data that Visage was designed to store.

You wish that this didn't happen, or that you could remove the log table, but you know that Siobhán has a lot of influence in the company, and she usually gets what she wants.

You urgently need a solution to handle this immense rate of incoming data on the Visage database server.

Antipattern: The Belief That You Need All Data

Aaron seems not to understand your concern about the rapidly growing database. He says he needs the data, and he has the support of a senior manager, so this isn't a problem as he sees it.

You'll have to explain the risks to him.

Problems with Unlimited Database Growth

There are several good reasons to be mindful of database growth, including the following.

Storage Capacity Has a Limit

The most urgent negative effect of database growth is that data will fill up your storage volume. Each row of data uses some storage space on average, and as you store more rows, the space they use is at least linearly proportional to the size of each row. If the storage fills to 100 percent, the database will deny insertion of new data, but it's even worse than that—PostgreSQL panics and shuts down completely, according to its documentation.[1]

If the storage fills up to that degree, all functions of the Visage application that touch the database will stop. Typically, this means the site will be down for all users, as engineers scramble to restore operation.

These days, many applications like Visage run on cloud systems, storage is virtual, and you have the option of expanding a storage volume if you need to. But this takes some time and requires authorization.

Applications that run on physical infrastructure have an even greater challenge because if a physical storage device is full, you either need to move the database content to a server with larger storage, or else refit the current database server with a larger storage device. Either of these solutions requires system administrator privileges and more time. The Visage site will remain down until this upgrade is completed.

Storage Costs Money

Any time you expand the database storage after unexpectedly reaching its limit will be an emergency expense, so you need to be able to justify it in the budget. You can increase capacity, as long as you can pay for it, but this might endanger the financial success of your company. Storage volumes for database servers are typically more expensive since they may be provisioned with cutting-edge hardware. In the cloud, they are often configured with high-performance options, which make them even more costly.

1. https://www.postgresql.org/docs/current/diskusage.html#DISK-FULL

Query Performance

The larger your database table, the more difficult it is to ensure good query performance, even if you have optimized with indexes. An index helps by turning an $O(n)$ search into an $O(\log n)$ search, but an algorithm with logarithmic complexity still increases as n increases.

Database Operations

Database operations such as schema changes are progressively more risky and time-consuming as databases get larger. Some schema changes with `ALTER TABLE` require a temporary copy of the whole table, so if the free storage space is less than the space needed for an extra copy of a given table, then you can't make a change like adding or dropping a column.

Backing up a database may take time proportional to the size of the database. A database that has unchecked growth eventually takes so long to back up that it can no longer be backed up once per day without the backup processes overlapping.

Aaron listens to all these warnings, and then suddenly his face lights up with an idea. "Let's add more database servers," he exclaims. "We'll store as much as we can on each server, and when one server fills up, we can store more data by switching it to the next server. About one month of `log` data will fit easily on a server, right? So, each month, we'll save new rows on the next server. In fact, we don't need to change the code every month—I can design the code once to do that automatically."

Aaron's proposal is called *sharding*.

What is Sharding?

Sharding is a strategy to define a table with the same name and columns on multiple database instances, and store a subset of rows—a *shard*—on each server. No row is stored on more than one server.

Think of sharding like a multivolume encyclopedia set. It would be impractical to make a single book with a binding large enough for all the content. So, an encyclopedia is split into a dozen or more volumes, each spanning a range of entries. You know how to find which book holds the entry you're looking for because they are stored in alphabetical order.

Aaron's proposal is to define the shards as split by the month and year of their creation date. Rows inserted `'2025-01-01'` through `'2025-01-31'` are stored on the first instance. Once the date proceeds to February 2025, rows inserted

'2025-02-01' through '2025-02-28' are inserted on the second instance. The third instance holds rows for '2025-03-01' through '2025-03-31', and so on.

The tables have the same structure on every instance, so a query against one instance will work against any instance. That query will return a distinct result from each instance.

Sharding spreads data out over more servers or spreads query traffic out over more servers. The goal is to scale out computing, memory, or storage resources to handle the growing demand.

Problems with Sharding

Aaron enthusiastically dives into implementing his sharding idea. For testing purposes, he starts three Docker containers on his local development workstation, each running an instance of PostgreSQL. Each instance needs to run on a distinct port, but otherwise they're all accessed via localhost.

Next, he creates a database named visage on each instance, with a table named log with an identical structure to the log table in production. He inserts one row into the table on each shard as a test so he can query the full set. The following simple shell script inserts the rows:

Sharding/shard-load.sh

```
psql -h localhost -p 5433 -U visage visage \
  -c "INSERT INTO log (log_id, log_type, log_data)
      VALUES (1, 10, '{\"data\": \"event on shard 1\"}')"

psql -h localhost -p 5434 -U visage visage \
  -c "INSERT INTO log (log_id, log_type, log_data)
      VALUES (2, 20, '{\"data\": \"event on shard 2\"}')"

psql -h localhost -p 5435 -U visage visage \
  -c "INSERT INTO log (log_id, log_type, log_data)
      VALUES (3, 30, '{\"data\": \"event on shard 3\"}')"
```

Now, he's ready to write some code.

Code Complexity

To use shards, an application needs a connection to each of the database instances. The SQLAlchemy framework for Python supports connecting to multiple databases by declaring a dict for a collection of connection properties. It refers to these as *binds*. In Visage, the declaration can be added to the Flask configuration mapping as shown in the code on the next page.

Sharding/anti/visage-logs.py

```
flask_app = Flask(__name__)
flask_app.config.from_mapping(
    SECRET_KEY="visage_key",
    SQLALCHEMY_DATABASE_URI="postgresql+psycopg2://localhost:5432/visage",
    SQLALCHEMY_ECHO=True,
    SQLALCHEMY_BINDS={
        "shard1": "postgresql+psycopg2://visage:xyzzy@localhost:5433/visage",
        "shard2": "postgresql+psycopg2://visage:xyzzy@localhost:5434/visage",
        "shard3": "postgresql+psycopg2://visage:xyzzy@localhost:5435/visage",
    },
)
```

Then, a method that queries a sharded table needs to query each respective instance. SQLAlchemy instances are accessed via the `db.engines` mapping. The following code for the `Log` model class shows a method that queries the instances in a loop and collects the results into a single array of rows. Once the results are unified, they are passed to the HTML view:

Sharding/anti/visage-logs.py

```
class Log(db.Model):
    __tablename__ = "log"

    log_id: Mapped[int] = mapped_column(primary_key=True)
    log_type: Mapped[int] = mapped_column(nullable=False)
    log_data: Mapped[JSON] = mapped_column(type_=JSON, nullable=False)
    created_at: Mapped[datetime] = mapped_column(
        default=lambda: datetime.now(timezone.utc))

    @staticmethod
    def query(query, shards=["shard1", "shard2", "shard3"]):
        results = []
        for shard in shards:
            with db.engines[shard].begin() as shard_db:
                shard_results = shard_db.execute(query).fetchall()
                results.extend(shard_results)
        return results

@flask_app.route("/logs")
def logs():
    logs = Log.query(
        db.select(Log.log_id, Log.created_at, Log.log_type, Log.log_data)
    )
    return render_template("logs.html",
                           logs=logs)
```

The following view displays the results it is given, with no regard to the fact that the rows originated on different shards:

Sharding/anti/templates/logs.html

```
<!DOCTYPE html>
<html>
```

```
<head><title>Visage Logs</title></head>
<body>
  <h1>Visage Logs</h1>

  <hr>

  <table border="1">
    <tr>
      <th>Log ID</th>
      <th>Created At</th>
      <th>Log Type</th>
      <th>Log Data</th>
    </tr>
    {% for log in logs %}
    <tr>
      <td>{{log.log_id}}</td>
      <td>{{log.created_at}}</td>
      <td>{{log.log_type}}</td>
      <td>{{log.log_data}}</td>
    </tr>
  {% endfor %}
  </table>

</body>
</html>
```

Aaron's first attempt to demonstrate querying across a sharded dataset produces the following output, which shows the three test rows Aaron inserted in the `log` tables:

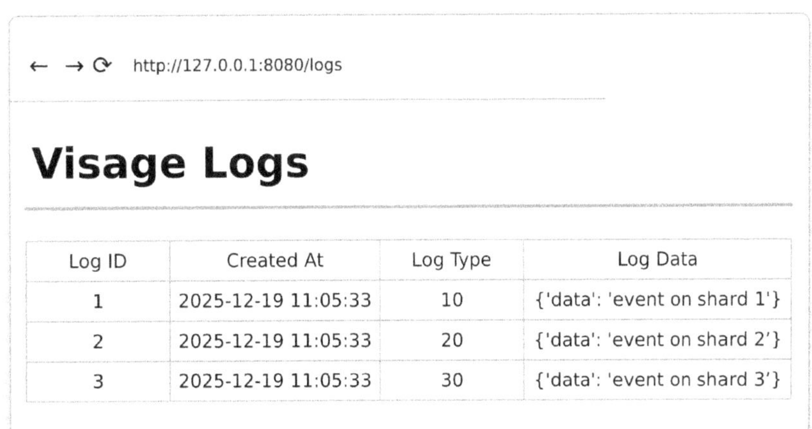

Log ID	Created At	Log Type	Log Data
1	2025-12-19 11:05:33	10	{'data': 'event on shard 1'}
2	2025-12-19 11:05:33	20	{'data': 'event on shard 2'}
3	2025-12-19 11:05:33	30	{'data': 'event on shard 3'}

Cross-Shard Queries

The first problem you and Aaron identify is that the view of logs seems to run slower than he expects. After all, as it queries the `log` table, it needs to run three queries, one for each shard. It's still examining the same total number of rows as if the data were colocated in a single database instance, but now the rows are split over several shards. But that's not the only cost of a query. Each query executed has some overhead costs, as the Python code loops over the set of connections, starts transactions, and sends a query to the database instance, where it is parsed, optimized, and executed. After the results from a given shard are fetched, they are appended to the collected results in the Python code. This is naturally more overhead than running a single query against a single database instance.

This is called a *cross-shard query* or a *fan-out query*. The problem is that it gets more costly the more shards you create.

Aaron considers whether there's a way to optimize this. "Depending on the query," he thinks out loud, "it wouldn't have to query *every* shard. If a query were searching only for matches in a single month, then it should touch only the shard that contains that month's data."

He tries to write code that analyzes the query before looping over shards, automatically inferring which shard(s) it needs to query. You and Aaron think of several potential ways of expressing conditions. The following queries would each need clever code to analyze the query syntax to infer the minimal list of shards they would search:

Sharding/anti/date-range-queries.sql

```sql
SELECT * FROM log
WHERE created_at BETWEEN '2025-06-01' and '2025-11-30';

SELECT * FROM log
WHERE created_at > '2025-06-01';

SELECT * FROM log
WHERE DATE_TRUNC('month', created_at) = '2025-11-01';

SELECT * FROM log
WHERE created_at > '2025-12-01' OR event_type = 20;
```

It's also clear that only queries with a condition on `created_at` even have a chance of reducing the set of shards to examine. All other queries are definitely cross-shard queries.

The task gets even more complex as you consider more complex cases like joins, subqueries, or common table expressions. Is there a way for the code to infer from any arbitrary query which shards it can avoid reading?

Eventually, Aaron has a sinking feeling. "Implementing this for any potential query is as much work as writing an SQL parser and semantic engine. I'll be duplicating the logic of the SQL query optimizer!"

Constraints Don't Work

The next problem appears after Aaron tries to add a few more rows of test data to each shard. He omits the primary key column from the INSERT statements to make the SERIAL primary key generate new values:

Sharding/shard-load-2.sh

```
psql -h localhost -p 5433 -U visage visage \
  -c "INSERT INTO log (log_type, log_data)
      VALUES (10, '{\"data\": \"event on shard 1\"}')"

psql -h localhost -p 5434 -U visage visage \
  -c "INSERT INTO log (log_type, log_data)
      VALUES (20, '{\"data\": \"event on shard 2\"}')"

psql -h localhost -p 5435 -U visage visage \
  -c "INSERT INTO log (log_type, log_data)
      VALUES (30, '{\"data\": \"event on shard 3\"}')"
```

After loading these rows, viewing the logs shows duplicates in the log_id values:

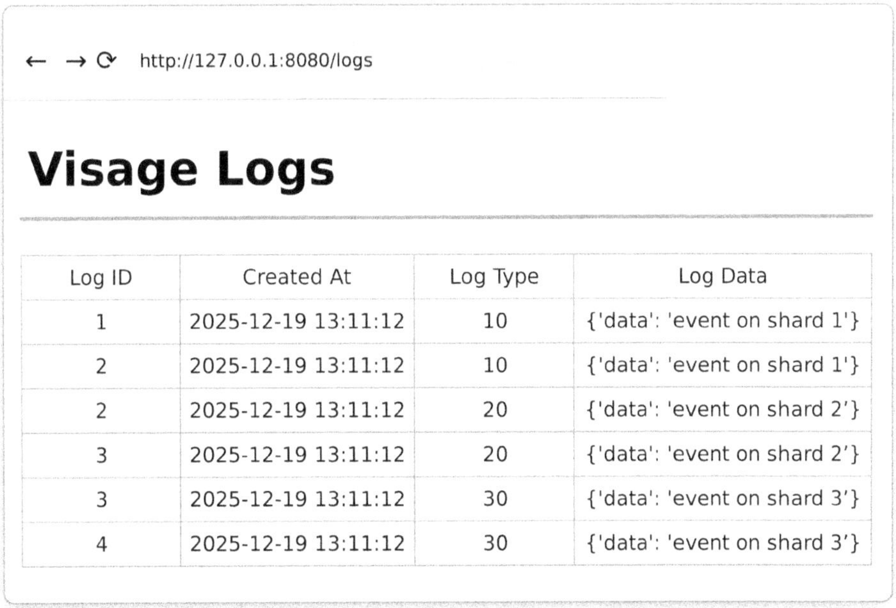

← → ⟳ http://127.0.0.1:8080/logs

Visage Logs

Log ID	Created At	Log Type	Log Data
1	2025-12-19 13:11:12	10	{'data': 'event on shard 1'}
2	2025-12-19 13:11:12	10	{'data': 'event on shard 1'}
2	2025-12-19 13:11:12	20	{'data': 'event on shard 2'}
3	2025-12-19 13:11:12	20	{'data': 'event on shard 2'}
3	2025-12-19 13:11:12	30	{'data': 'event on shard 3'}
4	2025-12-19 13:11:12	30	{'data': 'event on shard 3'}

Aaron is briefly surprised, but he quickly understands what happened. "Each shard has its own sequence of ID values," he explains. "They generated new values, one greater than the row that exists in the same shard, but they don't know about values that exist in other shards."

The shards don't generate ID values that are unique with respect to the whole collection. If they were to coordinate among all the other instances, it would require them to have a protocol to prevent generating the same ID value when clients insert to different shards concurrently. This protocol would briefly lock the table on every shard while the next ID is generated.

Aaron suggests using a UUID type as the primary key instead of a SERIAL. A UUID or Universally Unique ID is a 128-bit value generated in a way that makes it very unlikely for concurrent processes to generate the same value. It's useful for exactly this case—when independent servers are generating values that need to be unique.

Sharding/anti/uuid.sql

```
SELECT uuidv7();

-- Example: 019b46d8-34c9-7076-b82c-f82606d3c130
```

But the more general problem still exists: in a sharded table, unique constraints and foreign key constraints are hard to enforce because, in both cases, they compare a given row to other rows in the collection. Since a sharded collection is split and distributed over several database instances, enforcing the constraint would likely require accessing all the other instances. This would again require some kind of cross-shard protocol, which would be a bottleneck for scalability.

Query Hotspots

Aaron defined the sharding by splitting the log table by date ranges, so each shard holds the data created during one month. But that means that all the new rows for log will be inserted to a single shard. Also, any queries for the log table tend to be for reports of recent data, so largely, they ignore shards holding older data.

The choice of the column to use for splitting the data—known as the *shard key*—can be responsible for this kind of imbalanced query traffic. Eventually, one shard has to serve more throughput than a single server can sustain, but if the traffic were distributed more evenly over the set of servers, then it would be possible.

Over time, this so-called *hotspot* may move from one shard to the next. Therefore, all the database instances must be provisioned on a powerful server, which later becomes underutilized. It's an expensive way to support growth.

You can think of other ways to choose the shard key to balance query traffic and make use of all the servers. Aaron decides he'll use the log_id column as the shard key. Adding new rows uses all the shards in a round-robin fashion.

This is a popular method of sharding because it keeps the shards approximately balanced. But any query for a date range will have to run a cross-shard query.

It's hard to choose a shard key that minimizes both cross-shard queries and hotspots.

Towers of Hanoi

Even with Aaron's balanced instances, they will eventually become overutilized, either in storage capacity or query throughput capacity. Then, it's time to add another instance. This process is called *resharding*, and it can take more work than you might expect.

For example, in Aaron's current approach, the shard for a given row is calculated as the modulus of its primary key value. When he adds a new shard, the modulus changes for many of the rows, so they need to be moved from their current shard to one of the others. This can take a long time if the shards are all storing a lot of rows already.

Aaron is still talking to himself, working through all the tasks he needs to write code for. "What if new rows need to be stored while the resharding is in progress? Do I need to block concurrent inserts, or can I insert new rows into their final destination shard? Hmm ... that means some rows exist on their new shard, but not all of them, so I can't easily run any reports until the resharding is done." He's typing furiously.

Resharding is also necessary if you change your mind about the shard key.

Parallel Evolution

Suppose Aaron wants to add a column to the log table to record the user who was responsible for a given log event. That's a typical ALTER TABLE operation, but in a sharded environment, it brings up a new challenge.

Sharding/anti/add-column.sql

```
ALTER TABLE log
  ADD COLUMN user_id BIGINT REFERENCES "user";
```

How can he run this table alteration on all shards simultaneously? He can write a multithreaded utility to start the alteration against all shards concurrently, but that doesn't guarantee the task will finish at the same time. Some shards may store more rows or be more heavily loaded with query traffic. Starting an alteration might be delayed on a given shard because of queries holding locks on the table.

One approach is to permit only schema changes that preserve backward compatibility. Adding a column is safe because application code can simply avoid referencing the new column until all shards have finished the alter. Queries that use a wildcard like SELECT * reference a new column immediately as it appears in an altered table, which causes confusion if the shards finish their alterations at different times; see the chapter "Implicit Columns" in *SQL Antipatterns Volume 1 [Kar22]* for more about this.

Can Databases Make Sharding Easier?

Aaron shares with you an article on the growing popularity of distributed SQL databases like CockroachDB,[2] TiDB,[3] or Google Spanner.[4]

Distributed databases implement sharding, and they automate some of the difficult problems described earlier in this chapter.

For example, a distributed database analyzes SQL queries so it can execute part of the query on one or more physical servers that store a respective subset of data. Then, the database collects the results from those partial queries and returns the final unified result set to your client application. They may also automate operations like resharding, schema changes, or backup and restore.

SQL databases like PostgreSQL or MySQL may use add-on frameworks to reduce the work of sharding. For PostgreSQL, open source options include Multigres[5] or Citus.[6] For MySQL, PlanetScale Vitess[7] is a popular solution.

These products help, but there are some database development tasks that they can't do for you.

The most significant example is choosing the shard key. Even if a distributed database is clever enough to run queries on multiple shards in parallel, it's always going to be more efficient to avoid cross-shard queries. This means you have to choose the shard key carefully, to ensure the queries you need to be most optimized are bound to execute on one shard at a time, but also avoid inadvertently creating hotspots.

---

2. https://www.cockroachlabs.com/
3. https://www.pingcap.com/
4. https://cloud.google.com/spanner
5. https://multigres.com/
6. https://www.citusdata.com/
7. https://planetscale.com/vitess

Another disadvantage of using a sharding framework is that constraints have limitations. For example, in Vitess, foreign keys are supported only if child rows and the parent rows they reference are stored on the same shard.

Stored procedures also have limitations if the procedure references a table that is sharded. Since a stored procedure executes in a single database instance, it can only read or write rows of data on the same instance.

Some businesses have tried to use sharding frameworks such as Vitess and have been disappointed. They hoped a sharded architecture would behave transparently as if it were a single database server, but in fact, the developers were forced to become experts in designing their tables and queries to avoid scalability weaknesses.

After experiencing all these consequences from trying to develop his sharding experiment, Aaron starts to doubt that it's a simple way to manage the rapidly growing `log` table.

How to Recognize the Antipattern

- "I got another alert about disk space on the database server running out. Can we get a server with bigger storage?"

  Expanding the storage capacity may be a short-term solution to postpone action, but you can't do this forever. You need a different strategy to prevent alerts.

- "We got this memo from the legal department upstairs that we need to retain all data indefinitely. Don't delete anything, ever."

  This order usually comes from people who don't understand how to calculate the cost of storing an ever-increasing collection of data, or how to manage the scalability of doing so. There needs to be a plan for how to accommodate the business needs in a responsible way.

- "What's the maximum number of rows in a table?"

  It's not a bad idea to know this limit, but if any tables are approaching the maximum number of rows, then you need a new scaling strategy.

Legitimate Uses of the Antipattern

This book focuses on databases used in OLTP (On-Line Transactional Processing) applications, like web apps. These are characterized by many concurrent sessions and frequent, quick transactions.

What *Is* the Maximum Number of Rows in a Table?

It's a common habit for developers to choose a 32-bit integer column as the primary key of a table.

```
CREATE TABLE mytable (id INT PRIMARY KEY);
```

If you start with id value 1 and never skip any values, the maximum number of rows in that table is 2^{31}-1, or 2,147,483,647. This has created the misconception that the maximum number of rows in *any* table is limited by the number of positive values in a 32-bit integer.

But this doesn't tell the whole story.

You should remember that you can define a primary key using other data types that support a much larger range of unique values, such as the following:

```
CREATE TABLE mytable (id BIGINT PRIMARY KEY);
CREATE TABLE mytable (id VARCHAR(50) PRIMARY KEY);
CREATE TABLE mytable (id UUID PRIMARY KEY);
```

You can also define primary keys over two or more columns, which would allow a larger number of distinct key values. The following example allows 2^{31}-1 rows per distinct value of shard, and there can be up to 2^{31}-1 values in shard.

```
CREATE TABLE mytable (shard INT, id INT, PRIMARY KEY (shard, id));
```

The true limit of rows per table depends on each product's implementation, but is almost always much higher than the range of positive values in a single 32-bit integer.

Databases used for OLAP (On-Line Analytical Processing), data warehousing, or data science have different usage patterns. These typically run less frequent transactions and have more tolerance for long-latency queries. They usually contain much larger collections of data than OLTP databases.

You still need to be mindful of infrastructure, but other uses of databases are more tolerant of less-than-perfect optimization. Because of the size of such databases, it may be necessary to scale out with sharded databases, even though some queries will become cross-shard queries.

Solution: An Intervention to Manage Data Retention

Aaron is now convinced that simply giving more storage capacity to the log table isn't the best solution. Adopting a sharded architecture leads to a lot of questions and more work that he wasn't expecting.

The next morning, he asks you to help him make a practical plan to avoid more urgent alerts about storage space being exhausted—without sharding.

Together, you come up with the following priorities.

Save Data with a Purpose

The simplest strategy is to stop being a data hoarder. Choose which data your application stores in the database according to known requirements, instead of storing too much by default just in case you think of a reason later.

Extreme programming, an agile software development methodology that started in the 1990s, popularized the phrase *you ain't gonna need it* (YAGNI). This describes a principle to implement features when you actually need them, not in anticipation of a need that might never occur.

It's tempting to compromise this principle, especially when it comes to data. If a question comes up suddenly that could be answered if you had, say, the last year's worth of records, it would be convenient to have that collection ready to analyze. Whereas if you don't start collecting data until the question comes up, then you can't answer the question with respect to history—only about how the trends develop from the time you begin collecting the data.

Nevertheless, keeping all data that might be needed is very expensive and makes your project more complex. It's usually a net positive to follow the YAGNI principle.

Practice Capacity Planning

If you do implement a system that saves a lot of data, then you should make it a priority to prevent the emergency condition. Make it a habit to monitor storage usage before it becomes an alert. You can measure how quickly the database is filling up its storage, and then estimate how long until the current storage volume is too full.

Add a chart like the example at the top of the next page to the system monitoring dashboard to track the last four weeks. Most software teams have a regular meeting, such as a sprint planning. Make it a regular item of the agenda to review charts like this, to make sure everyone on the team using this infrastructure is aware of its capacity and how their product is using it.

Project the rate of increase into the future, and estimate the date you expect to be alerted if you don't take action. This tells you the outer limit of how long you have.

Document the process, the budget, and the lead time needed to provision infrastructure, and potentially migrate databases or code to it. Then agree on what action you need to take, and set the schedule for when to take action.

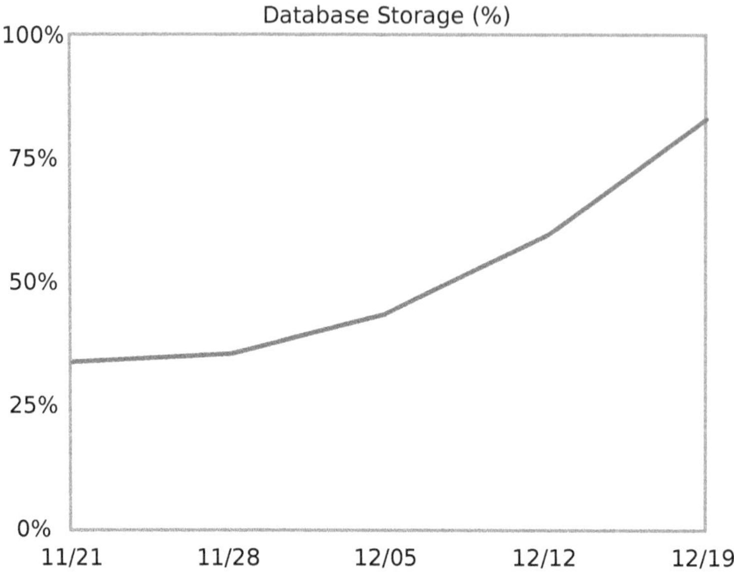

Implement an Archiving Strategy

Not all data are in equal demand. An OLTP database contains data on a sliding scale of most valuable to least valuable. Think of a chatroom application, for example. The most valuable data are typically the most recent, and they are queried frequently. Older data quickly become less in demand and are queried less and less.

In Chapter 10, Cacheless Transactions, on page 121, you read about optimizing access to frequently read data by keeping it in a cache. The complementary strategy is to move seldom-read data to another form of storage, so the database stays small enough to have good performance.

The first step is to define the criteria for which data must be kept in the database. This may be difficult. Some voices might insist that *all* the data must be accessible instantly. But this is seldom true in an OLTP database (if it truly is, then you might in fact need another database for OLAP-style work).

The second step is to decide what to do with the data you move out of the database. There are several choices:

- Move data to a secondary database instance that is also accessed by your application.
- Move data to a data warehouse, which is not accessed by your application, but is used by reporting tools.

- Back up data and keep the backup in cold storage. This is not accessible by any interactive tools, but it's still recoverable by request. This is appropriate if you have a legal or financial requirement to preserve data.
- Summarize data. For example, older records could be replaced by aggregate statistics like subtotals and counts.
- Finally, delete the data. If it's too low-value to be interesting to anyone, then why keep it at all?

Monitoring the rate of new data creation gives you a target for how much you need to archive.

Plan Sharding Carefully

"Hypothetically, if we had decided to use sharding, what would be the best shard key?" Aaron asks the rhetorical question with a smile on his face. Based on what you observed with Aaron during his experiments, the choice of shard key depends on many factors.

The primary influence on your shard key is the set of queries you need to have optimized so that you can avoid cross-shard queries as much as possible. But it's common to have a variety of query types in a given application, and they can't all be optimized when your data is sharded.

Other problems to consider are keeping query traffic balanced and keeping the rate of growth balanced. These could demand a different choice of shard key.

You might also want to optimize for simplifying the process of resharding when it occurs.

Or you might even want the most efficient task to be archiving data.

Any of these criteria might be the most important for your application. Therefore, there's no single choice that is the *best* shard key—but there may be one or more choices that have strengths that satisfy the requirements of your application, while the inevitable weaknesses aren't deal-breakers.

Aaron realizes that it'll take time to plan out a sharding strategy. It's more important right now to address the growth of the `log` table he created.

Make It Boring

After you and Aaron agree on a plan to manage database growth proactively, you decide it's best to postpone sharding. You're not going to have your pager alerting you about storage space too soon.

It's a good idea to reduce risks where possible. Your goal should be to minimize surprises and emergencies by monitoring database growth and making it predictable.

You should focus on being innovative and taking risks only when the upside of those risks results in more business value for your project.

This Isn't Really a Technical Problem

It's simpler, more economical, and easier to implement a policy to archive, summarize, or delete data, so you should try those strategies first. Unfortunately, in some organizations, deciding on that policy is much harder than implementing it.

Someone must be willing to decide which data need to be in the primary OLTP database, and which can be offloaded to cold storage. The people who know the data and queries well enough to make that judgment often aren't the ones with the authority to approve that action, and vice versa. No one wants to take needed data out of the database, and there may be interested parties who need access to any given subset of the data—or at least they don't know that they *won't* need those data, so they advocate to retain all the data.

Sharding is usually not the best technical solution, but it's the only technical solution you can implement without consensus.

Maintain stable performance by moving data out of the database at least at the same rate as you insert new data.

Any intelligent fool can make things bigger, more complex, and more violent. It takes a touch of genius—and a lot of courage to move in the opposite direction.

E. F. Schumacher

CHAPTER 15

Wrapping Up

That's all the SQL antipatterns for this book. There are, of course, more antipatterns, but I hope these are the most common, and therefore, it will do the most good if you can recognize and avoid them.

Let's wrap up with a few general observations.

Optimization Is About Priorities

You can't optimize all types of SQL queries simultaneously; you're always faced with trade-offs. That means you'll be making decisions about the priorities of the queries (or any other part of your code). Even if you make no choice, that sets a de facto prioritization.

Making priorities in an intentional way is a process that most of us have no training in, so it may feel like guesswork. How do you know what the options are? How do you evaluate or measure priority? How can you defend your decisions if your manager or anyone else in your team questions them?

If you're interested in learning professional methods of defining priorities, a recommended resource is Harry Max's book *Managing Priorities: How to Create Better Plans and Make Smarter Decisions. [Max24]*

Expand Your Toolbox

Advance your knowledge of SQL to help you develop code faster, as well as develop faster code.

Learn about how to use complementary technologies such as a cache or a message queue, and practice in order to understand how to decide when each of these is the best solution for a given performance goal.

Use monitoring dashboards to track the resource usage of your application and its database so you can get actionable information about the causes of performance bottlenecks.

You can develop wisdom partly from study and education, but it also comes from experience and practice.

Think Holistically

It's good to think outside the box and test alternative solutions.

When using denormalization, JSON documents, or NoSQL, you'll find that some types of optimizations commit you to a trade-off you didn't want. You may be giving up data integrity or losing flexibility to run different types of queries.

Finding the right balance of optimization is important. Using modest optimization for a broad range of queries can be better than the highest optimization if the latter harms too many other cases.

Be Prepared for Questions

We know that optimization of one query comes at the expense of other queries. This is nice for users of the former query, but the others also have users. When those queries are needed, you will be asked *why aren't they optimized?*

This is when you need courage to justify your earlier choice about which query you prioritized. It will be small consolation to those users inconvenienced because the query they need today isn't the one you optimized. They may even be the same individuals who yesterday demanded that you optimize the former query.

Be calm and patient. Explain again the reasons that those choices were made. Offer to refactor the software to optimize differently, since priorities sometimes change. But if you made the earlier choice well, then you can defend it more confidently.

Signing Off

Thank you for reading my book.

My wish for you is that you get the chance, from time to time, to do some work you're proud of.

A is for updates of two or three
C is for constraints that must agree
I is how I preserve what I see
D will save to disk to eliminate a fatal risk

APPENDIX 1

ACID Transactions

ACID is an acronym. It refers to a set of four properties needed for transactions: *Atomicity*, *Consistency*, *Isolation*, and *Durability*.

The importance of ACID for a database can be shown if we consider what the database would fail to do if it were not to support each of these properties.

Atomicity

Suppose you make multiple updates in the database. These updates may have a necessary grouping; there will be problems if any client can view the data after one update is applied without the other updates.

The textbook example is a bank transfer where you debit funds in one account, then credit the same amount in another account. If you had to commit the first update independently of the second update, it could briefly leave the accounts in a state that seems to show a debit without the matching credit. Someone might think their money had disappeared.

If the second update fails, for example, if the application crashes before it commits the second update, this would be an even worse problem. The discrepancy would be permanent, instead of brief.

Atomicity is the solution to these problems. A transaction defers commit until all the related updates have succeeded. If any of them fail, you have the option to roll back the whole set of updates, reverting the data to its state at the start of the transaction.

A database that doesn't support atomicity wouldn't be able to support such changes reliably.

Consistency

SQL constraints like FOREIGN KEY or UNIQUE KEY ensure data integrity. When you execute a change in the database, the data must satisfy all constraints before and after your transaction. For example, to satisfy a foreign key constraint, if a child row references a parent row, that parent row must exist.

Another example is that when using a cascading foreign key, updating a key value in a parent row cascades to any rows that reference it.

In some databases, it's allowed for constraints to postpone enforcement until the transaction commits. In other cases, the constraint must be satisfied immediately when each INSERT, UPDATE, or DELETE executes. PostgreSQL allows you to set the behavior of each constraint.

If the database doesn't support consistency, it may support *eventual consistency*. That is, suppose you update a key value that is referenced by cascading foreign keys. After your update, the referencing child rows aren't updated immediately. They will be updated soon, but until then, a client can read child rows that still have the old value.

In these circumstances, you can't rely on constraints always being satisfied. This means a JOIN won't return a parent row joined to its child rows because the value in the child rows doesn't match. If you repeat the same query with JOIN a moment later, then the eventual consistency has been applied to child rows, and the query returns a different result.

Some NoSQL databases rely on eventual consistency, achieving better performance by deferring some of the work of an update. This might be desirable, especially in a distributed database where the child rows exist on a different server. If the database engine has to search for child rows among several servers, it causes more overhead and could delay the commit of the update to the parent table.

Isolation

You don't want other clients to see the data you are in the process of updating until your transaction is committed. This means your changes are isolated.

If the database doesn't support isolation, it means other clients may see partial updates you are making in your session. For example, your change consists of multiple updates, and you want to commit them atomically.

Some databases support transactions with an isolation level of READ_UNCOMMITTED, which allows sessions to query partial updates. Use of this isolation level isn't often recommended. It causes confusion because a client doesn't know if your session has completed its updates. Also, that client doesn't know if your session will commit the updates. Their session might read data in a state that will be reverted when you roll back.

Durability

Once you commit a data change and the database reports success, you expect the change to remain intact. Even if the server suffers a sudden crash and restart, the last change you made to the data should not be undone. This is what's known as durability.

A database that reports that a change was successful before the change has been saved to durable storage is, in a way, lying. If the server crashes, that data change could be lost.

Real durability requires the database engine to wait for the storage to save data. We saw in Numbers Everyone Should Know, on page 126 that storage is orders of magnitude slower than memory, so it's tempting to compromise durability to avoid that delay.

Many NoSQL databases are not durable. Instead, they may store multiple copies of data on different instances. They assume that it's less likely for multiple instances to lose exactly the same data due to crashes, so they think this is sufficient for them to claim that the data has been saved.

ACID Is a Good Thing

The four ACID properties provide safeguards that make database transactions reliable and coherent. Sacrificing these properties increases risk and complexity.

The Programmers' Credo: we do these things not because they are easy, but because we thought they were going to be easy.

@Pinboard

APPENDIX 2

The CAP Theorem

Since 2002, computer scientists have agreed that a distributed data store cannot have all three of the following qualities:

- *Consistency*: you can read updated data immediately after you update.
- *Availability*: when you request to read data, it responds without delay.
- *Partition tolerance*: the distributed database, with a subset of its data on different servers, will work even when the network occasionally hiccups.

If you want partition tolerance (that is, a distributed database), then you have to choose which is more important, consistency or availability.

If you sacrifice consistency, then your query might read from a part of the database that hasn't processed the update, and will return data that doesn't include the most recent change.

If you sacrifice availability, then your query might have to wait until the partition has processed the update, or else the query might be canceled if it can't read the latest data immediately.

A traditional relational database on a single server has the first two qualities, consistency and availability, sacrificing partition tolerance. It's tricky for an SQL database to do something like enforce a UNIQUE constraint when it must check data on more than one partition to do that. If the network between these partitions is temporarily not working, then that constraint can't be validated (at least not without an unacceptable delay).

CAP is most important if the network is susceptible to interruption, for example, a wide-area network. In a controlled environment where the network is more reliable (that is, no network hiccups), the risk of network partitioning is low. The related *PACELC theorem*[1] says that even when the system is

1. https://www.cs.umd.edu/~abadi/papers/abadi-pacelc.pdf

working normally, a trade-off exists between latency and consistency. Prioritizing consistency ensures that updates over a distributed database are atomic, but this requires some time for synchronization. If the system instead prioritizes low latency, it must give up strong consistency guarantees and use asynchronous updates (eventual consistency).

NoSQL databases that work as a distributed database have chosen different priorities than a relational database. This is why NoSQL distributed databases are eventually consistent—they don't guarantee to read the most recent data immediately after an update.

The CAP and PACELC theorems remind us that every type of optimization comes with trade-offs. Any solution could be right for a given application, but none are right for all applications. It's up to you to understand your application's priorities, so you can pick the architecture whose strengths support the needs of your application.

Bibliography

[AF15] Martin L. Abbott and Michael T. Fisher. *The Art of Scalability: Scalable Web Architecture, Processes, and Organizations for the Modern Enterprise.* Addison-Wesley Professional, Boston, MA, 2nd Edition, 2015.

[Atk24] Andrew Atkinson. *High Performance PostgreSQL for Rails.* The Pragmatic Bookshelf, Dallas, TX, 2024.

[Bea20] Alan Beaulieu. *Learning SQL.* O'Reilly & Associates, Inc., Sebastopol, CA, 3rd Edition, 2020.

[BMMM98] William J. Brown, Raphael C. Malveau, Hays W. McCormick III, and Thomas J. Mowbray. *AntiPatterns.* John Wiley & Sons, New York, NY, 1998.

[Bra11] Ronald Bradford. *Effective MySQL Optimizing SQL Statements.* McGraw-Hill, Emeryville, CA, 2011.

[Cod70] Edgar F. Codd. A Relational Model of Data for Large Shared Data Banks. *Communications of the ACM.* 13[6]:377–387, 1970, June. https://doi.org/10.1145/362384.362685

[Dym15] Alexander Dymo. *Ruby Performance Optimization.* The Pragmatic Bookshelf, Dallas, TX, 2015.

[Gla92] Robert L. Glass. *Facts and Fallacies of Software Engineering.* Addison-Wesley Professional, Boston, MA, 1992.

[Kar22] Bill Karwin. *SQL Antipatterns, Volume 1.* The Pragmatic Bookshelf, Dallas, TX, 2022.

[Kim13] Ralph Kimball. *The Data Warehouse Toolkit: The Definitive Guide to Dimensional Modeling.* John Wiley & Sons, New York, NY, 3rd Edition, 2013.

[KOH22] Kevin Kline, Regina O. Obe, and Leo S. Hsu. *SQL in a Nutshell: A Desktop Quick Reference.* O'Reilly & Associates, Inc., Sebastopol, CA, 4th Edition, 2022.

[KR26] Martin Kleppmann and Chris Riccomini. *Designing Data-Intensive Applications.* O'Reilly & Associates, Inc., Sebastopol, CA, 2nd Edition, 2026.

[Mag25] Denis Magda. *Just Use Postgres!: A fast guide for developers* . Manning Publications Co., Greenwich, CT, 2025.

[Max24] Harry Max. *Managing Priorities: How to Create Better Plans and Make Smarter Decisions.* Two Waves Books, https://rosenfeldmedia.com/two-waves-books/, 2024.

[Mih16] Vlad Mihalcea. *High-Performance Java Persistence.* Vlad Mihalcea, Cluj, Romania, 2016.

[Nic21] Daniel Nichter. *Efficient MySQL Performance.* O'Reilly & Associates, Inc., Sebastopol, CA, 2021.

[SACL79] P. Griffiths Selinger, M. M. Astrahan, D. D. Chamberlin, R. A. Lorie, and T. G. Price. Access Path Selection in a Relational Database Management System. *SIGMOD '79: Proceedings of the 1979 ACM SIGMOD international conference on Management of data.* 23 - 34, 1979. https://doi.org/10.1145/582095.582099

[Vie18] John L. Viescas. *SQL Queries for Mere Mortals: A Hands-On Guide to Data Manipulation in SQL.* Addison-Wesley, Boston, MA, 4th Edition, 2018.

[Win12] Markus Winand. *SQL Performance Explained.* Markus Winand, Vienna, Austria, 2012.

Thank you!

How did you enjoy this book? Please let us know. Take a moment and email us at support@pragprog.com with your feedback. Tell us your story and you could win free ebooks. Please use the subject line "Book Feedback."

Ready for your next great Pragmatic Bookshelf book? Come on over to https://pragprog.com and use the coupon code BUYANOTHER2026 to save 30% on your next ebook.

Void where prohibited, restricted, or otherwise unwelcome. Do not use ebooks near water. If rash persists, see a doctor. Doesn't apply to *The Pragmatic Programmer* ebook because it's older than the Pragmatic Bookshelf itself. Side effects may include increased knowledge and skill, increased marketability, and deep satisfaction. Increase dosage regularly.

And thank you for your continued support,

Dave Thomas

SQL Antipatterns, Volume 1

SQL is the ubiquitous language for software developers working with structured data. Most developers who rely on SQL are experts in their favorite language (such as Java, Python, or Go), but they're not experts in SQL. They often depend on antipatterns—-solutions that look right but become increasingly painful to work with as you uncover their hidden costs. Learn to identify and avoid many of these common blunders. Refactor an inherited nightmare into a data model that really works. Updated for the current versions of MySQL and Python, this new edition adds a dozen brand new mini-antipatterns for quick wins.

Bill Karwin
(378 pages) ISBN: 9781680508987. $47.95
https://pragprog.com/book/bksap1

Designing Data Governance from the Ground Up

Businesses own more data than ever before, but it's of no value if you don't know how to use it. Data governance manages the people, processes, and strategy needed for deploying data projects to production. But doing it well is far from easy: Less than one fourth of business leaders say their organizations are data driven. In *Designing Data Governance from the Ground Up*, you'll build a cross-functional strategy to create roadmaps and stewardship for data-focused projects, embed data governance into your engineering practice, and put processes in place to monitor data after deployment.

Lauren Maffeo
(100 pages) ISBN: 9781680509809. $29.95
https://pragprog.com/book/lmmlops

Seven Databases in Seven Weeks, Second Edition

Data is getting bigger and more complex by the day, and so are your choices in handling it. Explore some of the most cutting-edge databases available—from a traditional relational database to newer NoSQL approaches—and make informed decisions about challenging data storage problems. This is the only comprehensive guide to the world of NoSQL databases, with in-depth practical and conceptual introductions to seven different technologies: Redis, Neo4J, CouchDB, MongoDB, HBase, Postgres, and DynamoDB. This second edition includes a new chapter on DynamoDB and updated content for each chapter.

Luc Perkins, Jim Wilson, Eric Redmond
(358 pages) ISBN: 9781680502534. $47.95
https://pragprog.com/book/pwrdata

High Performance PostgreSQL for Rails

Build faster, more reliable Rails apps by taking the best advanced PostgreSQL and Active Record capabilities, and using them to solve your application scale and growth challenges. Gain the skills needed to comfortably work with multi-terabyte databases, and with complex Active Record, SQL, and specialized Indexes. Develop your skills with PostgreSQL on your laptop, then take them into production, while keeping everything in sync. Make slow queries fast, perform any schema or data migration without errors, use scaling techniques like read/write splitting, partitioning, and sharding, to meet demanding workload requirements from Internet scale consumer apps to enterprise SaaS.

Andrew Atkinson
(454 pages) ISBN: 9798888650387. $64.95
https://pragprog.com/book/aapsql

The Pragmatic Bookshelf

The Pragmatic Bookshelf features books written by professional developers for professional developers. The titles continue the well-known Pragmatic Programmer style and continue to garner awards and rave reviews. As development gets more and more difficult, the Pragmatic Programmers will be there with more titles and products to help you stay on top of your game.

Visit Us Online

This Book's Home Page

https://pragprog.com/book/bksap2

Source code from this book, errata, and other resources. Come give us feedback, too!

Keep Up-to-Date

https://pragprog.com

Join our announcement mailing list (low volume) or follow us on Twitter @pragprog for new titles, sales, coupons, hot tips, and more.

New and Noteworthy

https://pragprog.com/news

Check out the latest Pragmatic developments, new titles, and other offerings.

Save on the ebook

Save on the ebook versions of this title. Owning the paper version of this book entitles you to purchase the electronic versions at a terrific discount.

PDFs are great for carrying around on your laptop—they are hyperlinked, have color, and are fully searchable. Most titles are also available for the iPhone and iPod touch, Amazon Kindle, and other popular e-book readers.

Send a copy of your receipt to support@pragprog.com and we'll provide you with a discount coupon.

Contact Us

Online Orders:	*https://pragprog.com/catalog*
Customer Service:	*support@pragprog.com*
International Rights:	*translations@pragprog.com*
Academic Use:	*academic@pragprog.com*
Write for Us:	*http://write-for-us.pragprog.com*

www.ingramcontent.com/pod-product-compliance
Lightning Source LLC
LaVergne TN
LVHW080453160826
845677LV00006B/1346

* 9 7 9 8 8 8 8 6 5 2 0 6 0 *